The Natural ROSE GARDENER

written by
Lance Walheim

major photography by
Scott Millard

illustrations by
Don Fox

IRONWOOD PRESS
TUCSON, ARIZONA

IRONWOOD PRESS

Publisher
Scott Millard

Associate Publisher
Eric A. Johnson

Business Manager
Michele V. M. Millard

Art Production
Paul Fitzgerald

Proofreading
Mary Campbell Nielsen

Indexing
Byliner

Typesetting
The Service Bureau

Printing 10 9 8 7 6 5 4 3 2

Printed in Korea by Sunprint

ISBN 0-9628236-3-5

Library of Congress Catalog Card
Number 94-075792

Cover photo: 'Fragrant Cloud', an
award-winning hybrid tea.

Title page photo: Pink 'Leander'
with red 'Margenrot'.

The information in this book is
true and accurate to the best of
our knowledge. It is offered
without guarantees on the part of
the author and the publisher,
who disclaim any liability in
connection with the use of this
information.

Address inquiries to:
IRONWOOD PRESS
2968 West Ina Road #285
Tucson, Arizona   85741

Dedication

This book is dedicated to Maxine Johnson for
her love of growing flowers, especially roses.

Photography
Elizabeth Ball
page 140 bottom left

Cathy Barash
page 13 bottom right

Michael Landis
cover, page 8 top left and right, 24
bottom right, 25 bottom right, 28
bottom left, 29 top right, 30, 31
bottom left, 32 bottom, 60 bottom,
61 top and bottom left, 68 top left,
72 top and bottom left, 73 top, 76
top left, 80 top and bottom left,
84, 88 top left, 89 top, 92 top, 96
top left, 100 bottom, 101 top right,
109 top left and bottom right, 117
top and bottom right, 121 bottom,
124 bottom left, 128 top right and
bottom, 133 top and bottom left,
137, 140 top, 141

Charles Mann
page 44 top right and bottom
right, 45 top, 49

Scott Millard
title page, pages 4, 5, 9, 13 top, 13
bottom right, 16, 17, 18, 19, 21, 22,
23, 24 right, 25 left, 26, 27, 28
bottom right and top right, 29
bottom right, 31 top left, 32 top
left and far right, 33 top right and
bottom right, 36, 37, 40, 41, 44 top
left and bottom left, 45 bottom
left and bottom right, 48, 52, 53,
57, 60 top left and top right, 61
bottom right, 64 top right, 68 top
right, bottom left and bottom
right, 69 top and bottom right, 72
bottom right, 73 bottom left, 76
top right, bottom left and bottom
right, 80 bottom right, 85, 88 top
right and bottom, 89 bottom, 93
top left and bottom, 96 top right
and bottom, 100 top, 101 top left
and bottom, 104, 105 top, 109 top
right and bottom left, 113 top left
and right, bottom right, 116, 117
bottom left, 120 top left and
bottom, 124 top and bottom right,
125, 128 top left, 136, 140 bottom
right, 144

Peter Rogers
page 29 bottom left, 31 bottom
right, 33 bottom left, 56, 64 top
left and bottom, 69 bottom left,
73 bottom right, 92 bottom left
and right, 93 top right, 105
bottom left and right, 108, 113
bottom left, 120 top right, 121 top
left and right, 133 bottom right

Mark Walheim
page 29 left, 31 top right, 32 top
right

Andy Wasowski
page 8 bottom

Special thanks to:

Maxine Johnson and
Michele V. M. Millard

For their assistance, thanks to:

All-America Rose Selections, Inc.
American Rose Society

Charles E. Basham,
Claremont, Calif.

Rita and Mel Bough,
Ft. Myers, Florida

Barbara and Larry Buster,
Muscatine, Iowa

Tom Carruth, Weeks Roses,
Upland, Calif.

Richard Hanlon,
Charleston, West Virginia

Paul Heard, Owen Memorial
Rose Garden, Eugene, Oregon

Jack and Heidi Jepson,
Tigard, Oregon

Daryl Johnson, International Rose
Test Garden, Portland, Oregon

Dr. Bill Nettles, Clinton, Michigan

The Phoenix Rose Society,
Phoenix, Arizona

Pixie Treasures miniature rose
nursery, Yorba Linda, Calif.

Steven Scanniello, Brooklyn
Botanic Garden, New York

Ernie Schultz, M.D.,
Rancho Palos Verdes, Calif.

Carol Shockley,
Conway, Arkansas

Lawrence J. Toole,
Little Silver, New Jersey

Sharon Van Enoo, Torrance, Calif.

Ashley and Teale Walheim,
Exeter, Calif.

Jan and Jack Weverka,
Monrovia, Calif.

Jon Wier,
Grand Rapids, Michigan

**Additional thanks goes to
the public rose gardens
and botanical gardens and
arboretums where many roses in
this book were photographed.**

Descanso Gardens Rose Gardens,
La Canada, Calif.

Huntington Library, Art
Collections and Botanical
Gardens, San Marino, Calif.

Owen Memorial Rose Garden,
Eugene, Oregon

Pageant of Roses Garden,
Whittier, Calif.

Planting Fields Arboretum,
Oyster Bay, New York

Portland International Rose
Garden, Portland, Oregon

Tohono Chul Park,
Tucson, Arizona

Tournament of Roses Wrigley
Garden, Pasadena, Calif.

Table of Contents

A NEW LOOK AT GROWING ROSES

How do you describe the timeless beauty of a rose, a flower so alluring and satisfying it has inspired poets, philosophers and artists for thousands of years? The Greek poet Sappho christened the rose "queen of flowers" over 2,500 years ago, and the rose still wears the crown today. No other flower evokes such meaning and emotion, with tens of thousands of plants and millions of cut flowers purchased and enjoyed each year.

When it comes to roses, great beauty can be blinding. Perhaps it's the nature of the rose blossom—the brilliant colors, the artistic way the petals unfurl, the hypnotizing fragrance—that causes the rose to be overlooked as an exceptional and versatile landscape plant.

Taking a Natural Approach

Providing a fresh look at the many ways roses can be used in the landscape is a primary goal of this book. Instead of considering roses only in traditional designs, the following pages offer more natural alternatives. Rather than a formal rose garden, plant free-flowering floribunda roses in an informal border, combined with your favorite perennials. Or grow old garden roses and allow them to naturalize on the perimeter of your property, creating a low-maintenance screen and wildlife habitat. Experiment with the new shrub roses in your landscape.

A second aspect of growing roses naturally is reducing or eliminating use of chemical controls for pests and diseases. Many gardeners today are seeking alternatives. Biological pest controls, insecticidal soaps and horticultural oils are some of the new controls available that are safer for the environment, as well as for the user. Rather than following a scheduled spray program, rose gardeners can now develop practices that prevent problems before they begin. The chapter "Planting & Care," pages 144 to 157, offers a complete discussion of ways to keep your roses growing and looking healthy.

Success with roses is no mystery; roses love to grow. Once they're established, most thrive with little care. Selecting disease-resistant varieties adapted to your climate region, planting properly and following preventive pest- and disease-control techniques will go a long way in making your rose garden a natural one.

Left: Roses and flowering plants are natural companions in the garden. Shown here are the English roses 'Redcoat' and 'Warwick Castle' with *Watsonia*.

Above: A sentiment from the past is a testament to the time-honored appeal of the rose.

The Rose's Rich History

To appreciate the significance of roses as garden plants, it helps to know a little of their extensive history. The early Romans were true lovers of roses. They carpeted their floors and showered their guests with rose petals, bathed in rose oils, drank rose wine, decorated warriors with rose garlands and treated their sick with medications made from rose petals and hips. When the supply of roses wasn't sufficient to meet demands, they built heated greenhouses so they could have flowers 12 months a year.

Evidence of the devotion given to the rose by early Christians is seen in stained glass windows in hundreds of medieval churches throughout the world. This tradition continues in modern churches today. Even the word *rosary*, a series of prayers reliving the life of Christ, originally meant *rose garden.*

Throughout history, from writings by Confucius several hundred years before the birth of Christ to England's War of the Roses in the 15th century, roses have been a part of world events. However, the roses that held such fascination long ago did not look much like the modern hybrid teas and grandifloras most of us grow today. The rose garden of Josephine, first wife of Napoleon, at Malmaison, their home in France, is still in existence. This garden contained almost 250 different roses, mostly rose species and natural hybrids. Quite a number of these roses are still in existence today, although they are not widely distributed through commercial outlets.

The Road to Modern Roses

The large collection of roses gathered by Josephine at Malmaison was an important step in the development of today's modern roses. For the first time, horticulturists could observe in one location the tremendous diversity of the rose family. From the Orient came everblooming *China roses* such as 'Parson's Pink China'. From Réunion, an island country in the Indian Ocean, came the semi-double, pink *Bourbon roses,* which were also everblooming. These were stunning in contrast to Europe's *Gallica roses,* which, although extremely fragrant, bloomed only in early summer.

Even though rose breeding had been going on for centuries, many of the roses displayed at Malmaison were natural hybrids and species found in nature. Consequently, the true lineage of many roses is uncertain and often confusing. Even still, horticulturists found the possibilities at Malmaison exciting. They began creating their own crosses, changing rose gardening forever. Hybrids between everblooming China roses and *Rosa moschata* led to the Noisette roses. At the same time, the hybrid perpetual was developed from mixed parentage. These were crossed with tea roses from China, resulting in the first hybrid tea rose. Soon, the era of modern roses was in full swing.

In North America, roses were also making an impact. There are approximately 200 species of roses worldwide. Of these, about 35 are native to the United States. As far back as the early 1600s, American Indians in the Northeast were planting roses to add flower color to their villages. Many native American roses, including *Rosa californica, Rosa setigera* and *Rosa palustris,* are rugged plants that are supremely adapted to the climates of their origins. In this current age of conservation when plants are required to thrive and look attractive with a minimum of care, as well as reduced amounts of water and fertilizer, these native American roses are ideal subjects.

In addition to native species, early settlers in North America also introduced many roses originating from other parts of the world. In the late 16th Century, William Penn, founder of Pennsylvania, brought 18 rose plants from England to the new world. He later wrote a book for pioneers about the value of roses as medicinal plants.

Old garden roses, as in the past, are enjoyed today for their fragrance, grace and beauty.

Roses in the 20th Century

Today, roses are big business. The rose is the world's most popular flower, and each year commercial rose growers produce millions of plants that are sold throughout the world. To meet the demand for new varieties, rose hybridizing and variety testing continue as important parts of the rose-growing process.

The Development of a Single Rose

Developing a new rose variety requires many years of evaluation and dedication. Take, for example, the 1990 All-America Rose Selection, 'Pleasure'. Like most other new introductions, 'Pleasure' was the result of 10 years of testing.

To get to this stage—a single, new rose—horticulturists for Jackson & Perkins Nursery evaluated almost 500,000 new seedlings. The best of these were planted in test plots across the country. (Many of these test roses can be seen at public rose gardens, labeled only with numbers.) The test plants were graded at regular intervals for every possible characteristic—from flower form to growth habit to disease resistance. By eliminating roses with undesirable traits, eventually only hybrids with exceptional characteristics remain. The few outstanding roses remaining are further evaluated for a two-year period by rose experts at over 20 All-America Rose Selection test plots around the country. Finally, the best of the best are named an *All-America Rose Selection* for that year.

New Directions in Rose Breeding

The late 1970s and 1980s brought important changes to rose gardening as breeders evaluated new hybrids. The changes in the kinds of roses that were being developed mirror an evolution in the way people want to garden.

In the past 40 years or so, the ultimate goal of many rose gardeners was simple: *grow the perfect flower.* As part of their quest, they followed an almost-weekly spray program to keep their plants free of insects and disease. However, as concern about pesticide safety increased, the number of safe but effective sprays on the market decreased. Many gardeners began to seek alternative ways to control pests.

Modern roses today, such as the hybrid tea 'Secret', are grown for their beauty as a cut flower, for rich fragrance and disease resistance.

Fortunately, one of the best means of pest and disease control is *prevention.* Preventing problems begins with selecting varieties of roses that are naturally resistant to attacks from common diseases. Problems with insect pests can be largely negated by allowing natural predator insects to prey on insect pests, reducing their populations. Prevention also means planting varieties and species that perform well in your climate and supplying them with proper care. Healthy roses—plants that are watered, fertilized and pruned properly—are much less prone to attacks from insects and disease.

Meanwhile, many gardeners became interested in the history and beauty of *antique* or *heritage* roses, such as the Damask and Bourbon roses. These old roses bring a different character to the garden, one that is less refined, but one that has a simple and natural elegance, blending with other plants in the landscape. They also have unique and interesting flowers, often with intense fragrance. As cut flowers, old roses seem to turn bouquets into works of early European art. In addition, wonderful new hybrids like the David Austin English roses are now being grown throughout North America. These roses combine the beauty of old varieties with the everblooming qualities of newer roses.

To meet the needs of the environmentally aware gardener, the vast majority of new rose hybrids are carefully evaluated for disease resistance. And, luckily for the landscape rose gardener, disease resistance usually translates into roses that possess attractive foliage as well as great versatility as landscape plants.

Above: An informal planting of climbing roses creates a relaxing and tranquil scene.

Above right: Roses are equally at home as part of a formal design, the rich flower colors standing out against the bright green of trimmed hedges.

Right: Chestnut rose, *Rosa roxburghii,* is striking trained on a rustic fence at this ranch near San Antonio, Texas. Midway back is pink 'Lavender Lassie' and behind is hot pink 'Vanity.'

Left: surrounded by roses, Sharon Van Enoo takes full advantage of a sunny afternoon in her back yard garden.

Below: Creating dramatic color combinations is one of the goals of rose grower Dr. Ernie Schultz. This combination includes white 'Iceberg' with red 'Guy Laroche', miniatures 'Redhot' and 'Pinstripe'. Flowering tree in the background is orchid tree, *Bauhinia variegata*; blue-flowering plant at right is pride of Madeira, *Echium fastuosum*.

Cold Temperatures
Average Minimum
Temperature for January

Albuquerque	34.1
Atlanta	44.0
Atlantic City	34.8
Baltimore	35.5
Boston	29.8
Charleston	49.9
Chicago	25.7
Dallas	45.8
Denver	32.0
Detroit	25.5
Houston	54.2
Kansas City	30.2
Las Vegas	44.6
Los Angeles	54.2
Memphis	42.3
Miami	68.0
Milwaukee	20.6
Minneapolis	13.1
Montreal	13.0
New Haven	29.7
New Orleans	53.5
New York	32.1
Philadelphia	34.4
Phoenix	51.8
Portland, ME	23.4
Portland, OR	39.4
Salt Lake City	30.1
San Francisco	49.8
Seattle	39.5
Toledo	26.9
Toronto	22.2
Tulsa	38.1
Vancouver	35.6

Source: *Climate and Man*

Climate-Wise Rose Gardening

Your region and its climate have a definite impact on almost every aspect of how your roses will grow. Climate can affect the color and substance of the flowers, as well as influence which pests and diseases are likely to be present to cause problems. Even the *survival* of roses in your garden can depend on your climate and the growing conditions of a particular site.

Average daily temperatures in summer, extreme low temperatures in winter, the amount of summer sunshine, atmospheric humidity and other factors influence which rose varieties perform best in your area. They also help determine timing and methods of planting, pruning and fertilizing. Getting to know your "climate ingredients" and gardening in tune with them are important aspects of being a natural rose gardener.

Sunshine

The amount of sun your garden receives during the growing season depends on several factors: the region where you live (your general climate zone), the direction of the garden's exposure (north, south, east or west) and the amount of shade cast by plants or structures on garden sites.

Roses grow best in full sun and should receive a minimum of six hours of direct sun each day. In hot-summer climates such as in the desert Southwest, too much sun can cause plants to sunburn and flowers to fade prematurely. Locations that receive afternoon shade can be a solution. It is also wise to time plantings so young plants are not stressed by hot summer temperatures. Plant bareroot roses so they'll have some time to establish before high heat comes on. If starting with roses in containers, plant in fall or early in spring. See page 148 for recommendations on when to plant in your area.

In cool, foggy climates, such as coastal regions and parts of the Pacific Northwest, *not enough* sunshine and heat can be a problem. It helps to plant in the sunniest locations in your garden—exposures that face south or west. If possible, take advantage of reflected heat and light from light-colored walls. See illustration, page 147. Also refer to "Climate and Rose Flowers," page 12.

Cold Temperatures

Every plant has a cold-temperature tolerance. When the temperature drops below this point for a certain period of time, plant tissues are damaged. How long cold temperatures last, how quickly they drop and the season when they occur affect the reaction of plants to the cold. If the drop in temperature is severe and occurs when plants are not hardened to the cold (early in fall or in spring when there is new tender growth), the plant is much more likely to suffer serious injury or death.

Most roses, however, are generally cold-hardy plants. Hybrid teas are the least cold hardy of the modern roses, although some hybrid teas are more cold hardy than others. Floribundas and polyanthas are slightly more cold tolerant than hybrid teas.

Many species roses, shrub roses and some old garden roses are cold hardy. Some shrub forms have been specifically bred for cold hardiness. See listing of plants on page 55. They can usually be grown successfully almost anywhere in the United States. Other old garden roses, such as the Chinas and Noisettes, are tender plants and best adapted to mild-winter climates.

Where temperatures fall below 10F to 20F, most roses need winter protection. A 6- to 8-inch mound of soil or mulch over the *bud union*—the location on the plant where the rootstock is grafted to the top growth—will usually suffice. In northern and high-elevation regions, where temperatures can fall well below 0F, additional protection measures will be required. See page 154 for methods.

Be aware that a drop in temperature is not the sole cause of winter damage. Drying winds, lack of soil moisture, intense sunlight and extreme fluctuations of warm and cold temperatures will adversely affect rose plants and their ability to tolerate the winter season.

Rainfall

The amount of rainfall your garden receives, particularly during the summer growing season, will of course affect how much you'll have to irrigate your roses. Average annual rainfall in the United States ranges from a few inches to 50 inches or more. Some gardeners seldom have to irrigate their roses; for others irrigation is the most important part of rose care. (Soil type also has a great effect on irrigation. See pages 148 to 150.)

Even if it seems that rainfall has been plentiful, it is difficult to judge how much moisture a rainstorm delivers to plant roots. This is particularly true with intense thunderstorms, where water can run off rather than soak into the soil. To determine the benefit of a rain, check the depth that moisture has penetrated the soil around your roses. Be careful not to injure the shallow surface roots. Look and feel the soil to see if plants can skip an irrigation.

Rain, like humidity, can also deter or encourage diseases and pests. If rains are frequent in your region, causing conditions to be moist and humid, expect some trouble with certain pests and diseases. See "Humidity," following, as well as the chart on pests and diseases, page 157.

Humidity

How does atmospheric humidity affect rose culture? For one thing, it affects availability of moisture to plants and the need for irrigation. In a high-humidity climate, evaporation of moisture, whether as rain or irrigation, is slow. Moisture remains in the soil to benefit plants for a longer period. With low humidity, evaporation of moisture can be quite rapid so little accumulates in the soil.

In addition, the level of humidity encourages certain diseases and pests. Black spot and powdery mildew flourish in humid, damp conditions. Likewise, spider mites are encouraged by a hot, dry environment. It is when conditions are extreme—with either very high or low humidity—that you should be most diligent in checking your roses for problems. Catching an infestation of insects or disease early makes controls, particularly natural ones, much more effective.

Wind

Good air circulation in the form of breezes and light winds is a benefit to rose gardeners. As air moves through and among plants, it causes moisture from the morning dew, irrigation and rainfall to evaporate from plant leaves and stems. This is why it is important to space plants properly—to allow enough room for air circulation to prevent diseases. But when winds are strong they can cause serious damage. High winds in summer desiccate (dry out) plants rapidly, and tear and tatter leaves and flowers. Winter winds also dry out plants, especially young ones, and can batter and injure rose canes when plants are dormant.

A windbreak planting may be required if you live in an area that commonly receives strong seasonal winds. Plant *semidense* evergreen trees or large shrubs— it's better that some breezes filters through or winds can crash down over the windbreak with great force. Study the direction of prevailing winds when winds are most damaging. Locate windbreaks perpendicular to these prevailing winds.

Microclimates

Within your general climate are numerous small climates called *microclimates*. Site topography, exposures, paved areas, structures and size and placement of plants create a broad range of growing conditions, from full shade to reflected sun and heat. Every home lot is different, and changes occur as plants grow on

Rainfall		
	July/ Aug.	Annual
Albuquerque	2.71	8.40
Atlanta	8.39	47.58
Atlantic City	8.36	40.91
Baltimore	9.12	41.94
Boston	6.55	38.94
Charleston	11.76	40.26
Chicago	6.40	31.85
Dallas	4.61	33.60
Denver	3.04	13.99
Detroit	5.81	31.04
Houston	8.24	44.84
Kansas City	7.43	35.73
Las Vegas	1.21	4.84
Los Angeles	.09	14.76
Memphis	6.14	45.29
Miami	11.66	59.18
Milwaukee	5.25	29.64
Minneapolis	6.70	27.31
Montreal	7.16	40.65
New Haven	7.45	44.96
New Orleans	12.92	59.72
New York	8.38	41.63
Philadelphia	9.10	41.86
Phoenix	1.93	7.62
Portland, ME	5.97	42.05
Portland, OR	1.14	39.43
Salt Lake City	1.48	15.79
San Francisco	.03	20.23
Seattle	1.29	31.80
Toledo	5.71	32.11
Toronto	5.68	32.33
Tulsa	7.08	38.38
Vancouver	5.77	58.65

Source: *Climate and Man*

the site and create more shade. Take a walk around your own home and observe for yourself—some areas are warmer, cooler, windier, sunnier than others.

As you get to know the small climates around your home, you'll see they offer the potential to grow rose varieties that normally do not do well in your area. For example, planting next to a warm, south-facing wall may provide just enough extra heat to open a deep red rose in a cool climate. Or planting a cold-tender rose such as *Rosa banksiae* in an area with extra protection may be just enough to get it through cold winters. You'll also notice that not all planting sites are created equal. Select sites with proper amounts of sunshine and without competition from trees and shrubs.

Climate and Rose Culture

All plants tend to grow and mature faster in warm-climate areas. Seasonal bloom cycles may not last as long as they would in cooler areas, but there is often less time between cycles. Faster growth and warmer weather also cause rose plants to require more frequent fertilization and watering to sustain the vigorous growth.

Areas with relatively mild winters can expect a longer season of bloom than in cold-winter climates. In parts of Southern California, for example, it is common to see roses blooming in December. By comparison, roses growing in the Midwest or East will have been dormant for months.

Diseases—Areas with cool, foggy summers, such as the Pacific Northwest, can always expect powdery mildew. Warm, humid climates, typical of the South and Florida, encourage black spot. Rust disease thrives in arid parts of the West, but is not as serious a problem elsewhere in North America.

Pests—Insect pests also have regional preferences so are often bigger problems in some areas than in others. Climate is a factor but not the only consideration. For example, Japanese beetles attack roses primarily in the eastern United States. Mountain ranges have so far prevented them from migrating into the western states. Spider mites thrive in the hot, dry summers of the West and are not nearly as troublesome where summer rains are common.

Climate and Rose Flowers

Where you live can have an effect on both the color and substance of rose flowers. In general, dark-colored, multipetaled varieties, particularly fully double, red roses like 'Mister Lincoln' or 'Chrysler Imperial', perform best in areas with warm nighttime temperatures. In cooler regions, the lack of heat usually prevents roses with these types of blooms to open fully. There are some exceptions, such as the hybrid tea 'Olympiad'. It is one of the few red-flowering hybrid teas that grows successfully in both warm- and cool-summer areas.

In cool-summer regions, varieties that have lighter flower colors and fewer petals are generally most reliable. In warm-summer regions, the blooms of these kinds of varieties tend to look faded and washed out. Bicolored roses such as 'Double Delight', 'Peace' and 'Granada' *blush* better—their colors blending together naturally—in areas with cool nights. Yellow or pink colors become more prominent. In warmer areas red flower colors become more and distinct.

Regional Roses

A useful guide to selecting roses adapted to grow in your climate is listed on pages 28 to 30. These roses are recommended by regional chapters and individual members of the American Rose Society, as well as local rose experts. Many recently introduced varieties, such as David Austin roses, have not been in cultivation long enough to be fully evaluated for these areas, but most perform well in a variety of locations. Public rose gardens in your region are additional sources of information, allowing you to view hundreds of rose varieties at one time. See the listing of "Public Rose Gardens," following.

Public Rose Gardens

This listing of public gardens in the United States are accredited by the organization, All-America Rose Selections. These gardens serve to showcase hundreds of varieties of roses, including AARS winners, through the past several years.

Visiting a public garden in your area provides an excellent opportunity to compare the form, color and fragrance of many roses at one time.

In addition to the AARS gardens on these pages, there are many public botanical gardens and arboretums that include roses among their plant collections. These, too, are well worth a visit.

Alabama

Birmingham—The Formal Rose Garden at Birmingham Botanical Gardens

Fairhope—Fairhope City Rose Garden

Mobile—David A. Hemphill Park of Roses; Battleship Memorial Park Rose Garden

Theodore—Bellingrath Gardens Rose Garden

Arizona

Glendale—Saguaro Historical Ranch Rose Garden

Phoenix—Valley Garden Center Rose Garden

Tucson—Gene C. Reid Park Rose Garden

Arkansas

Little Rock—State Capitol Rose Garden

California

Citrus Heights—Fountain Square Rose Garden

Corona del Mar—Roger's Gardens

La Canada—Descanso Gardens Rose Garden

Los Angeles—Exposition Park Rose Garden; Watts Senior Citizen Center Rose Garden

Oakland—Morcom Amphitheater of Roses

Palos Verdes Peninsula—James J. White Rose Garden

Pasadena—Tournament of Roses Wrigley Garden

Riverside—Fairmont Park Rose Garden

Sacramento—Capitol Park Rose Garden; McKinley Park Rose Garden

San Diego—Inez Parker Memorial Rose Garden

San Francisco—Golden Gate Park Rose Garden

San Jose—San Jose Municipal Rose Garden

Santa Barbara—A.C. Postel Memorial Rose Garden

Westminster—Westminster Civic Center Rose Garden

Whittier—Pageant of Roses Garden

Colorado

Littleton—War Memorial Rose Garden

Longmont—Longmont Memorial Rose Garden at Roosevelt Park

Connecticut

Norwich—Norwich Memorial Rose Garden

Stratford—Boothe Park Wedding Rose Garden

West Hartford—Elizabeth Park Rose Garden

District of Columbia

Washington, D.C.—The George Washington University

Florida

Lake Buena—AARS Display Garden at Walt Disney World

Largo—Sturgeon Memorial Rose Garden

Winter Haven—Florida Cypress Gardens

Georgia

Athens—Elizabeth Bradley Turner Memorial Rose Garden

Atlanta—Atlanta Botanical Rose Garden

Thomasville—Thomasville Nurseries Rose Test Garden

Hawaii

Kula, Maui—University of Hawaii

Idaho

Boise—Julia Davis Rose Garden

Illinois

Alton—Nan Elliott Memorial Rose Garden at Gordon F. Moore Community Park

Evanston—Merrick Park Rose Garden

Glencoe—Bruce Krasberg Rose Garden at Chicago Botanic Garden

Libertyville—Lynn J. Arthur Rose Garden at Cook Memorial Park

Peoria—George L. Luthy Memorial Botanical Garden

Rockford—Sinnissippi Rose Garden at Rockford Park District

Springfield—Washington Park Rose Garden

Indiana

Ft. Wayne—Lakeside Rose Garden at Lakeside Park

Richmond—Richmond Rose Garden at Glen Miller Park

Iowa

Ames—Iowa State University Horticultural Gardens

Bettendorf—Charles Liebestein Memorial Rose Garden

Davenport—Vander Veer Park Municipal Rose Garden

Des Moines—Greenwood Park Rose Garden

Dubuque—Dubuque Arboretum Rose Garden

Muscatine—Weed Park Memorial Rose Garden

State Center—State Center Public Rose Garden

Kansas

Topeka—E.F.A. Reinisch Rose Garden

Kentucky

Louisville—Kentucky Memorial Rose Garden

Louisiana

Baton Rouge—Burden Research Plantation AARS Rose Garden

Many—Hodges Gardens

Shreveport—American Rose Center

Maine

Portland—City of Portland Rose Circle, Deering Oaks Park

Massachusetts

Boston—James P. Kelleher Rose Garden

Westfield—Stanley Park

Michigan

East Lansing—Michigan State University Horticulture Gardens

Minnesota

Chanhassen—Palma Wilson Rose Garden at Minnesota Landscape Arboretum

Minneapolis—Lyndale Park Municipal Rose Garden

Mississippi

Hattiesburg—Hattiesburg Area Public Rose Garden at University of S. Mississippi

Jackson—Jim Buck Ross Mississippi Agriculture and Forestry Museum Rose Garden

Missouri

Kansas City—Laura Conyers Smith Municipal Rose Garden at Jacob L. Loose Memorial Park

St. Louis—Gladney & Lehmann Rose Gardens at Missouri Botanical Gardens

Montana

Missoula—Missoula Memorial Rose Garden

Nebraska

Boys' Town—Boys' Town Constitution Rose Garden at Father Flanagan's Boys' Home

Lincoln—Lincoln Municipal Rose Garden at Antelope Park

Omaha—Memorial Park Rose Garden

Nevada

Reno—Reno Municipal Rose Garden

New Hampshire

North Hampton—Fuller Gardens Rose Gardens

New Jersey

East Millstone—Rudolf W. van der Goot Rose Garden at Colonial Park

Lincroft—Lambertus C. Bobbink Memorial Rose Garden at Thompson Park

Tenafly—Jack D. Lissemore Rose Garden at Davis Johnson Park & Gardens

New Mexico

Albuquerque—Prospect Park Rose Garden

New York

Bronx—The Peggy Rockefeller Rose Garden at New York Botanical Garden

Brooklyn—Cranford Rose Garden at Brooklyn Botanic Garden

Buffalo—Delaware Park Casino, and John Fuzak Memorial Rose Garden, Erie Basin Marina

Canandaigua—Sonnenberg Gardens Rose Garden

New York—United Nations Rose Garden

Old Westbury—Old Westbury Gardens

Rochester—Maplewood Park Rose Garden

Schenectady—Central Park Rose Garden

Syracuse—E.M. Mills Memorial Rose Garden at Thornden Park

North Carolina

Asheville—Biltmore Estate

Clemmons—Tanglewood Park Rose Garden

Fayetteville—Fayetteville Rose Garden at Fayetteville Technical Community College

Raleigh—Raleigh Municipal Rose Garden

Winston-Salem—Reynolds Rose Gardens of Wake Forest University

Ohio

Akron—Stan Hywet Hall and Gardens

Bay Village—Cahoon Memorial Rose Garden

Columbus—Columbus Park of Roses

Mansfield—Charles E. Nail Memorial Rose Garden

Youngstown—Fellows Riverside Gardens

Oklahoma

Muskogee—J.E. Conrad Municipal Rose Garden

Oklahoma City—Charles E. Sparks Rose Garden

Tulsa—Tulsa Municipal Rose Garden at Woodward Park

Oregon

Coos Bay—Shore Acres Botanical Garden/State Park

Corvallis—Corvallis Rose Garden at Avery Park

Eugene—Owen Memorial Rose Garden

Portland—International Rose Test Garden

Pennsylvania

Allentown—Malcolm W. Gross Memorial Rose Garden

Hershey—Hershey Gardens

Kennett Square—Longwood Gardens

McKeesport—Garden Club of McKeesport Arboretum at Renziehausen Park

Philadelphia—The Morris Arboretum Rose Garden at University of Pennsylvania

West Grove—Robert Pyle Memorial Rose Garden

South Carolina

Orangeburg—Edisto Memorial Gardens

South Dakota

Rapid City—Rapid City Memorial Rose Garden

Tennessee

Chattanooga—Warner Park Rose Garden

Memphis—Memphis Municipal Rose Garden

Texas

Austin—Mabel Davis Garden at Zilker Botanical Gardens

Dallas—Samual-Grand Municipal Rose Garden

El Paso—El Paso Municipal Rose Garden

Fort Worth—Fort Worth Botanic Garden Rose Garden

Houston—Houston Municipal Rose Garden

Tyler—Tyler Municipal Rose Garden

Utah

Fillmore—Territorial Statehouse State Park Rose Garden

Nephi—Nephi Federated Women's Club Memorial Rose Garden

Salt Lake City—Municipal Rose Garden

Virginia

Alexandria—All-America Rose Selections Garden

Arlington—Bon Air Memorial Rose Garden at Bon Air Park

Norfolk—Norfolk Botanical Gardens Bicentennial Garden

Washington

Bellingham—Fairhaven Rose Garden at Fairhaven Park

Chehalis—City of Chehalis Municipal Rose Garden

Seattle—Woodland Park Rose Garden

Spokane—Manito Park-Rose Hill

Tacoma—Point Defiance Rose Garden

West Virginia

Huntington—Ritter Park Rose Garden

Moundsville—The Palace Rose Garden

Wisconsin

Hales Corners—Boerner Botanical Gardens

Madison—Olbrich Botanical Gardens

LANDSCAPING WITH ROSES

Which roses will give you the most enjoyment year after year? How can you select those that will be the most colorful in the landscape? Which combine with other flowering plants? This chapter, including the numerous lists it contains, provides answers to these questions and many others.

With so many choices available, selecting the right roses is not always simple. The roses that will perform best for you will largely depend on the type of gardener you are, your personal preferences for color, fragrance and so on, and your climate. For instance, if you are a beginner, or if you prefer not to use chemical sprays, easy-to-grow or disease-resistant varieties might be best. Fragrance in a rose is also a matter of opinion. Some people prefer roses with a spicy or fruity fragrance; others prefer the musky aroma common to many red hybrid teas.

Roses have a new place in today's home landscape, a landscape that is becoming more informal and natural in appearance—a reflection of the lifestyle of today's gardener. To explore the possibilities, it helps to step back from the rose flower for a moment. Now look at the rose as a *landscape plant*. Measure a free-blooming floribunda such as 'Iceberg' or 'Sarabande' against any popular flowering shrub, including azalea, viburnum, camellia, hydrangea and hibiscus. For length of bloom and abundance of flowers, roses surpass any of these fine plants. Add in the appeal of crisp, clean foliage, cold hardiness, diverse growth habits and great vigor, and it becomes clear that the rose is one of the most versatile landscape plants available.

We hope this chapter provides you with some new ideas for using roses. To help get you started with your selections, turn to the "Rose Selection Guide," lists of roses organized by handy categories, pages 28 to 35.

Left: Noisette rose 'Madame Alfred Carrière' combines with 'Sally Holmes', a shrub rose, to make an all-white statement.

Above: Perennials, sundial and natural grouping of roses create a colorful scene.

Roses in the Landscape

The beauty of the rose flower is undeniable. People are drawn to the flowers, to see them close-up and to sample their fragrance—whether the flower is on the plant or in the vase. Perhaps this is one reason roses have been underutilized as landscape plants: People have a difficult time standing back and appreciating their landscape value.

However, interest in roses as landscape subjects is growing. Rose breeders have developed varieties that emphasize landscape qualities: handsome form, disease-resistant foliage, long season of bloom and low-maintenance growth characteristics. Meanwhile, a number of time-honored roses such as 'Betty Prior' and 'Sarabande' already possess these qualities. With a new following, they are finding their rightful place in the landscape.

How you choose to use roses in the landscape greatly depends on your personal preferences and gardening style. But there are sound guidelines to help you achieve your goals. It's usually not enough to consider only how roses relate to each other. Successful landscape designers study how all plants interact in terms of color, texture and form. Many plants, including flowering annuals, perennials and shrubs, can be used to highlight the best features of roses, making their display all the more dramatic. Roses can work equally well in a support role, emphasizing the unique qualities of landscape plants nearby. For example, the long bloom period and white flowers of 'Iceberg' make an excellent background for flowering perennials.

Selecting Roses by Color

One of the most important factors in using roses successfully is selecting flower colors carefully. There is beauty in simplicity, and one of the most effective uses of landscape roses involves combining several plants of a single hue. When roses are in full bloom, they are quite dramatic and demand attention. If too many colors are mixed together, the effect can overpower a garden. Still, a creative blend of rose varieties similar in flower color (as well as plant form), such as several shades of pink, can be stunning.

As you make your color choices, consider how colors can vary according to the surroundings and location of your garden. Walls, buildings, garden structures, background plants and even the sky *absorb* or *reflect* color. This affects the look of the garden. For example, light-colored flowers planted against a white wall lose much of their impact. Against a dark brick wall, the same flowers would capture and hold the viewer's attention.

The quality and degree of light vary according to where you live. Pastel and light-colored flowers tend to have the greatest impact in the cool, even light of the coastal garden. In the sun-drenched desert, these colors lose their intensity. The bright, warm-colored sunlight is better suited to rich reds, oranges, purples, magentas and yellows. And in woodsy areas of the South, Midwest and East, light yellows, pinks and whites appear softer and more at home in the filtered light of canopy trees.

For a garden that evokes calmness, select and mass plants with complementary foliage colors and textures and similar flower colors. An example of this would be 'Bonica' roses with pink-flowering geraniums. Place plants in natural-shaped drifts rather than a smattering of dribs and drabs. The idea is to blend colors as well as forms and textures together. This works especially well in small gardens, where simple plant combinations visually expand the garden space.

For a dynamic effect, create eye-catching combinations with *color opposites*. A good example is yellow roses planted with blue-violet salvia. If in doubt about certain color combinations, test them on a small scale by planting roses in containers, possibly using one rose variety for each container. This way you can see how colors combine with other flowering plants before putting roses in the ground.

Below left: Large miniatures and floribundas, primarily in shades of pink, act as flowering shrubs along driveway near home entrance.

Below: A climbing 'Cécile Brunner' trained on an overhead lattice helps create an inviting and secluded garden oasis.

When selecting colors of rose flowers, be aware your climate can have an impact—sometimes subtle, sometimes dramatic—on the actual color of the rose variety. See page 12 for more information.

Plant Form

When roses are a permanent part of the landscape, they serve as *structural plants*, functioning as screens, hedges, backgrounds and members of permanent borders. When used as such, consider how they will affect the landscape's appearance through the seasons. When plants are in bloom, they will have a dominant presence, but when they are between flowering cycles or when they are pruned in winter, their impact will be greatly diminished.

To avoid garden "downtime," combine roses with flowering plants that will be in bloom (attracting attention) when roses are not in their prime. Summer-flowering perennials or foliage plants located at the base of roses or behind them put on a show through the middle of the growing season—when most roses are between bloom periods. For winter interest, include evergreen plants such as azaleas, firs or rhododendrons as part of the landscape scheme to maintain the structure of the garden. Spring-blooming bulbs or wildflowers provide color early in the year.

Plant form is also determined by a plant's basic shape. Many roses have a rounded form, although climbers, many old roses and even some hybrid teas and floribundas, are certainly more spreading or upright. Plants with round forms combine especially well with plants that have upright or spiky flowers, such as hollyhock, delphinium, campanula, lavender, penstemon and salvia.

Plant Texture

Texture can mean different things in a landscape design. Close-up, it describes the surface of the leaves and flowers, such as fine-textured, lacy or coarse. It can also relate to the entire landscape scene as viewed from a distance, when the form of plants appears fine, coarse or a combination of the two. Because of the impact texture has on the entire scene, the leaves of *evergreen* plants are important and should be included in your design, since foliage is on display when the rose flowering season has passed.

Rose plants can have a range of textures, depending on type, variety and time of year. When not in bloom, stiff stems and dark foliage present a coarser texture, although some old roses and miniatures are finer foliaged. When in bloom, many roses, especially shrub roses, rugosas, floribundas and climbers, take on finer textures, although hybrid teas can remain quite coarse. Some roses, most notably the rugosas, have coarse-textured, crinkled foliage. They are dramatic additions to the garden in or out of bloom.

As you would blend colors, you can create blends of plants with similar textures. This could be as simple as mixing miniatures with floribundas. For contrast, use fine-textured plants in combination with coarse-textured roses. Examples include many ornamental grasses, santolina, lobelia and penstemon.

Rose Partners

Plants that combine well with roses are almost endless. After gaining a basic understanding of color and texture, only your imagination can limit the beautiful combinations you can create. To get some ideas flowing, here are some classic combinations and other plants that will complement your roses. It is important, however, to select companion plants that have similar cultural requirements, particularly in regard to their water need. Plants having like soil, sun and water needs will grow healthier and require less of your time to maintain.

Covering the bases—Many shrub roses remain full foliaged, with leaves all the way to the ground. Other rose forms, particularly hybrid teas and upright

floribundas, tend to become sparse near the base, especially late in the season. Miniature and polyantha roses can often be used in front of these roses to conceal the bare spots and add color of their own. Tight-growing, compact varieties like 'Beauty Secret', 'China Doll' and 'Yellow Doll' are ideal. For other suggestions, see "Roses for Edgings," page 33.

Other low, compact or spreading perennial plants that work well in front of roses include: white-flowering silvery yarrow, *Achillea clavennae*; pink-flowering sea pinks, *Armeria maritima*; yellow-flowering basket-of-gold, *Aurinia saxatilis*; one of several low-growing types of campanula, available in a range of colors; dianthus, also available in many colors; pink-, red- or magenta-flowering hardy geraniums; white, pink or red coral bells, *Heuchera* species; white-flowering candytuft, *Iberis sempervirens*; and pink- or blue-flowering moss pinks, *Phlox subulata*.

Some tidy annuals to consider include pink, purple or white sweet alyssum, *Lobularia maritima*; blue lobelia, *Lobelia erinus*; and petunias, pansies and violas, which come in a wide range of colors.

Roses and Herbs

Roses have a long history in the herb garden, where for centuries their flowers were gathered with pungent herbs to make potpourri, their oils distilled to make perfumes, and their hips collected to brew healthful tea. Old roses or species roses such as autumn damask, rugosas and 'Old Blush' China rose are appropriate selections from a historical perspective, but any fragrant variety fits in the herb garden.

Some good-looking herbs (there are many) excellent for planting with roses include southernwood, *Artemisia abrotanum*; foxglove, *Digitalis purpurea*; lavender, *Lavandula* species; purple or yellow sage, *Salvia* species; lemon or silver thyme, *Thymus* species; santolina, *Santolina* species; rosemary, *Rosmarinus* species; and scented geraniums, *Pelargonium* species.

Above left: Miniature roses make an interesting ground cover in combination with blue lobelia and lavender ground morning glory.

Above right: Siberian iris in the foreground helps "cover the bases" of hybrid tea 'Touch of Class.' Red valerian, *Centranthus ruber*, adds its complementary shades of rosy pink in the background.

Blue salvias, with their spiked flowers, make a striking combination with David Austin rose 'Lilian Austin'.

Classic Combinations

Certain plants, or types of plants, just seem to fit naturally with roses, looking better in combination than they do by themselves. Among them are gray-foliaged plants, which work to throw a spotlight on white, pink or red roses. They include: dusty miller, *Centaurea cineraria* and *Senecio cineraria*; santolina, *Santolina chamaecyparissus*; lamb's ears, *Stachys byzantina*; and artemisia, *Artemisia* species.

Plants with spiked flowers or dramatically upright or fountain-shaped habits contrast particularly well with the more mounded form of most roses. The deep blue flower spikes of gentian sage, *Salvia patens*, take on wonderful richness when planted with red- or pink-flowering roses. Combine it with the salmon pink polyantha 'Margo Koster', and the two plants take on regal hues. Gentian sage also goes well with white and yellow roses. Other spiky plants to try with roses include iris; red valerian, *Centranthus ruber*; lavender, *Lavandula* species; and garden penstemon, *Penstemon gloxinioides*.

Ornamental grasses make elegant companions for roses throughout the growing season. Purple fountain grass, *Pennisetum setaceum* 'Cupreum', with its purplish brown foliage and purple plumes, is stunning alongside pink-flowering 'Simplicity' or crimson 'Othello'. It can also be planted with red or white roses. The wispy plumes of feather grass, *Stipa gigantea*, come alive, dancing in the slightest breeze in front of the pink-flowering David Austin rose 'Gertrude Jekyll'.

A large selection of summer-flowering plants complement blooming roses. Perhaps more important, they put on a show of their own when roses are between bloom periods. These include annuals such as zinnia, cosmos and vinca. Many summer-flowering perennials are well suited to the rose garden. Several *Salvia* species; daylilies, *Hemerocallis* species; and summer phlox, *Phlox paniculata*, are just a few.

Climbing Roses

Climbing roses may be the best thing that can happen to a bare fence or wall. Trained along a fence, they add beautiful, long-lasting color available from few other plants. Perhaps the most classic example is using a red-flowering climber such as 'Blaze' on a white picket fence. However, climbing roses improve the appearance of any fence, whether it is made of chain-link or split rail.

Climbing roses grown against light-colored walls can be particularly dramatic. 'Altissimo' and 'Dortmund' are favorites to train this way. Attach thin wires stretched between screw-eyes mounted into the wall for supports, and the plants become living tapestries of exquisite color. Because climbing roses do not climb or cling like a vine, you must attach the canes or branches to the supports. This can be done easily by using garden ties or cotton string to hold main branches or canes. Another popular support against walls is a lath trellis. Climbing roses can also be trained to posts and arbors.

When you select a climbing rose variety make sure its vigor matches the size of its support. Restrained varieties are best for low fences or narrow walls. More vigorous roses require sturdy arbors or tall fences. Refer to the descriptions on pages 136 to 143.

Mass Plantings

Low-growing shrubs, floribundas and miniatures are ideal when planted en masse, forming a solid bed of color. Spaced about two feet apart, they create an effective ground cover or eye-catching focal point in the landscape. Select plants carefully, because roses have a wide range of mature heights, especially miniatures. Planting several plants of a single variety is one method to maintain consistency in height and plant form.

Many vigorous, old roses, including some of the Bourbons and hybrid perpetuals, can be *pegged* to increase their bloom when planted to cover large areas. To peg a rose, bend the tip of a long cane down and secure it with a stake and tie. For more information on old garden roses, see pages 40 to 55.

Above left: The flower colors of miniature rose 'Poker Chip' blend beautifully with that of Floribunda 'Gingersnap'.

Above right: It is important to consider the background color when selecting climbing roses. Choose a dark-flowering variety such as 'Dortmund', shown above, to train against light-colored walls. Likewise, a climber with light-colored flowers such as 'White Dawn' would be best suited to a dark background. Red rose in foreground is 'Othello', a David Austin English rose.

Below: 'Starina' miniature roses are at home in this rustic wood container, adding a welcome splash of color to the deck.

Below right: 'Remy' miniature rose works well in a hanging container. Be aware that container plants require frequent watering during warm weather—as often as every day in hot-summer regions.

Roses in Containers

With a well-draining potting soil, regular moisture and fertilizer, almost any rose can be grown in a container. However, compact-growing floribundas and miniatures provide the most color and are best adapted to the limited root space. Large containers, at least five-gallon size, are best. Half-barrels, available at nurseries and home centers, are popular for growing roses and many other plants. Be aware that they can be heavy and difficult to move after planting. Smaller pots allow you to stage your rose show wherever you want, positioning plants so their beauty can be enjoyed on patios, decks and entryways—wherever a splash of color is desired. But the smaller container size will necessitate more frequent watering.

Plant roses in a high-quality potting soil. Many commercial brands are available in bags at nurseries and garden supply stores. These soils possess the right combination of aeration and moisture-holding capacity necessary for long-term healthy growth. It is possible to mix up your own potting soil, but it takes time and is hard work. Members of your local chapter of the American Rose Society often have their own favorite potting soil recipes.

Soil polymers, dry, water-absorbing granules, can be added to your potting mix to decrease watering frequency. They can absorb hundreds of times their volume in water. By retaining water in the plants' root zones for a longer period, they help decrease the need for frequent watering. You can find them at most nurseries.

With each irrigation, make sure the water is thoroughly wetting the rootball and not washing down the sides of the container. If the pot is very dry (it will feel light when you tilt it), you may have to add water to the top of the container several times before the soil is completely moistened. Roses growing in containers will dry out much faster than those growing in the ground. Frequent watering is necessary, especially during summer.

Tree Roses

Tree roses are popular varieties of hybrid teas, floribundas and miniatures budded (grafted) to special, tall, straight-stemmed rootstocks. Tree roses have an air of

formality that can be attractive when several are used to line a drive or walkway or to frame an entry. Their height places the flowers closer to eye level where they can easily be enjoyed. Tree roses can also be used as backgrounds to shrub or perennial borders and in containers on patios and decks.

However, use tree roses in the landscape with discretion. In the wrong location or if over-used, their unusual and dramatic effect can make them appear out of place. If a natural or informal mood is your goal, consider another rose form.

Roses in Perennial Borders

One of the most exciting ways to use generous-blooming floribundas such as 'Iceberg' and 'Simplicity', shrub roses like 'Bonica' and the David Austin English roses, and polyanthas like 'The Fairy' is to plant them as foundation shrubs in mixed perennial borders. Placed in the border, they provide continuous color, highlighting flowering perennials as they come in and out of bloom. See photo below.

Many old roses and species roses are welcome additions to a perennial border, but some varieties bloom only once or twice during the season. Select ones that have desirable qualities such as repeat bloom, dramatic foliage and a restrained growth habit. For example, varieties of *Rosa rugosa* provide vibrant flower color, and their crisp, clean foliage looks good through the growing season.

Old Roses

As a group, old roses represent great variety in plant form, foliage and flower. Many are vigorous plants that can cover large areas or climb up into the canopies of trees. Others are compact, well-behaved specimens that fit neatly in small areas. Some old roses bloom only once a year in spring while others bloom several times during the season.

The diversity among old roses means you should choose them carefully for locations within your landscape. However, the same diversity also presents great opportunities. Many old roses possess beauty that is hard to find in modern roses. See page 40 for descriptions of more than 100 species and varieties.

Below left: 'Iceberg' floribunda is one of the most popular roses to use in combination with perennials. The white flowers can be planted with any color, and the bloom period is exceptionally long. Here it is planted with Jerusalem sage, *Phlomis fruticosa*.

Below: Tree roses in contrasting colors and sizes make interesting accents in a narrow planter.

Climbing old roses can be trained to climb over a trellis, arbor, post or high fence. Canes can be tied to sturdy supports with flexible garden ties available in nurseries, or they can be woven around the structure. More prostrate old roses like *Rosa wichuraiana* can be used as ground covers, on slopes for erosion control or as large-scale background plants. Their vigorous habits fit best in a more natural garden than in a setting having stronger lines and greater formality. Compact old roses like varieties of *Rosa rugosa* make good hedges. The growth rate and eventual height of the plant will influence the extent of pruning, as well as the mature size of the hedge.

Shrub Roses

No group exemplifies the evolution of roses as landscape plants more than modern shrub roses. Until 1987, when 'Bonica' was introduced, no shrub rose had been honored as an All-America Rose Selection. Since that time, two other shrub roses have been selected: 'All That Jazz' and 'Carefree Wonder'. Both are excellent landscape plants that are free-blooming, disease resistant and vigorous. Combined with the David Austin English roses (see pages 51 to 54), the Meidiland roses and others, they represent a versatile group that can be used as hedges, and in containers and mixed in perennial borders.

'Old Blush,' also known as 'Parsons' Pink China', sets the stage for this peaceful garden scene. For information on this rose, see page 47.

Left: 'Carefree Wonder', an All-America Rose Selection in 1991, is a popular and reliable landscape rose.

Below: David Austin English roses work well in the natural rose garden, here combining with flowering perennials. Shown are 'Redcoat' (left), 'Warwick Castle' (low-growing in center), 'Lucetta' (tall in background), and 'Lilian Austin' (right).

Rose Selection Guide

The lists on the following pages are designed to help you select the roses you want, whether you're seeking roses for fragrance, of a certain color or for disease resistance. Also refer to "Gallery of Roses," pages 36 to 143, for photographs and detailed descriptions of rose varieties.

Hardy Roses for Cold Climates

This list of varieties includes Rose Society recommendations from cold-climate states, including Michigan, New York, Illinois, Iowa, Colorado, West Virginia and New Jersey. Each of the varieties listed was recommended in at least two states.

Hybrid Teas
American Spirit
Chrysler Imperial
Double Delight
First Love
Fragrant Cloud
Garden Party
Granada
Medallion
Mister Lincoln
Olympiad

'Medallion' hybrid tea

Pascali
Peace
Pristine
Sheer Bliss
Summer Dream
Swarthmore
Tiffany
Touch of Class
Tropicana

Floribundas
Betty Prior
China Doll
Class Act
Europeana
Eye Paint
The Fairy
Gene Boerner
Iceberg
Impatient
Ivory Fashion
Little Darling
Sexy Rexy
Showbiz
Simplicity
Sunsprite

Grandifloras
Aquarius
Gold Medal
Love
Pink Parfait
Pristine
Queen Elizabeth
Tournament of Roses
Tropicana
White Lightnin'

Miniatures
Black Jade
Figurine
Judy Fischer
Magic Carrousel
Party Girl
Rise 'n' Shine
Simplex
Snowbride
Starina

Climbers
Altissimo
America
Blaze
Don Juan
Dortmund
Golden Showers
Handel
New Dawn

Shrubs
All That Jazz
Bonica
Carefree Wonder

Roses for Hot, Dry Climates

These roses are recommended by the Tucson, Arizona, Rose Society.

Top-Performing Hybrid Teas
Brandy
Chrysler Imperial
Double Delight
First Prize
Honor
Olympiad
Paradise
Peace
Royal Highness

Other Recommended Hybrid Teas
Chicago Peace
Color Magic
Dainty Bess
Fragrant Cloud
Garden Party
Granada
Miss All-American Beauty
Mister Lincoln
Mon Cheri
Oklahoma
Oregold
Peace
Summer Sunshine
Swarthmore
Sweet Surrender
Tiffany
Touch of Class

Grandifloras
Aquarius
Arizona

'Color Magic' hybrid tea

'French Lace' floribunda

Gold Medal
Montezuma
Olé
Queen Elizabeth
Shreveport
Sonia
Sundowner
White Lightnin'

Floribundas
Angel Face
Cherish
Europeana
French Lace
Gene Boerner
Gingersnap
Iceberg
Impatient
Intrigue
Ivory Fashion
Marina
Redgold
Sun Flare
Sunsprite

Miniatures
Beauty Secret
Cupcake
Dreamglo
Holy Toledo
Judy Fischer
Kathy
Lavender Jewel
Magic Carrousel
Mary Marshall
Minnie Pearl
Over the Rainbow
Pacesetter
Party Girl

Peaches 'n' Cream
Puppy Love
Rainbow's End
Rise 'n' Shine
Sheri Anne
Simplex
Snow Bride
Starina
Yellow Doll

Climbers
America
Don Juan
First Prize climber
Handel
Joseph's Coat
Lady Banks rose
Piñata
Queen Elizabeth climber
Tempo

'Chicago Peace' hybrid tea

Roses for Warm, Humid Climates

This list comes from rose societies in the Deep South, including Florida, Georgia and Alabama.

Hybrid Teas
Chicago Peace
Dainty Bess
Double Delight
First Prize
Fragrant Cloud
Friendship
Granada
Honor
Ivory Tower
Lady X
Mikado

Miss All-American Beauty
Mister Lincoln
Olympiad
Paradise
Pascali
Peace
Perfect Moment
Perfume Delight
Pristine
Rio Samba
Royal Highness
Tiffany
Touch of Class
Tropicana
Unforgettable
White Masterpiece

Floribundas
Angel Face
Apricot Nectar
Betty Prior
Cherish
China Doll
Class Act
Europeana
Gene Boerner
Iceberg
Impatient
Ivory Fashion
Redgold
Rose Parade
Sun Flare
Sunsprite

Grandifloras
Gold Medal
Love
Montezuma
Queen Elizabeth
Shining Hour
Sonia
Tournament of Roses

Miniatures
Black Jade
Child's Play

'Impatient' floribunda

'Piñata' climbing rose

Figurine
Loving Touch
Old Glory
Rise 'n' Shine
Winsome

Climbers
Altissimo
America
Don Juan
Dortmund

Shrubs
All That Jazz
Carefree Wonder

Roses for Cool-Summer Climates

This list of recommended rose varieties comes from the International Rose Test Garden in Portland, Oregon. Those marked with an asterisk are considered disease resistant.

Hybrid Teas
Color Magic
Dainty Bess
Folklore
Fragrant Cloud*
Heirloom
Honor
Just Joey*

'Iceberg' floribunda

Las Vegas
Medallion
Olympiad*
Paradise
Pascali*
Peace*
Precious Platinum
Princess Margaret
Pristine
Sheer Elegance
Tiffany
Touch of Class
Voodoo*

Floribundas
Amber Queen
Betty Prior
Class Act*
Europeana*
Eye Paint*
French Lace*
Iceberg*
Little Darling
Marina
Playboy*
Playgirl*
Redgold
Regensberg
Sarabande*
Sexy Rexy
Showbiz*
Simplicity
Sun Flare
Sunsprite
Trumpeter*

Grandifloras
Caribbean
Gold Medal
Love*
Prominent
Queen Elizabeth*
Tournament of Roses

Climbers
Altissimo
Dortmund*
Dublin Bay*
Golden Showers
Handel*
Joseph's Coat

Miniatures
Beauty Secret
Cinderella
Holy Toledo*
Little Artist*
Little Jackie
Magic Carrousel
Minnie Pearl
Party Girl
Rise 'n' Shine
Simplex*
Starina*

Shrubs
All That Jazz
Bonica
Carefree Wonder
Golden Wings
Graham Thomas

'Showbiz' floribunda

'Dortmund' climbing rose

Roses for Coastal Southern California

These roses were recommended by Tom Carruth, hybridizer-horticulturist for Weeks Roses, a wholesale rose nursery in Upland, California. For hot, inland areas of Southern California, refer to "Roses for Hot, Dry Climates," page 28.

Hybrid Teas
Anastasia
Brandy
Brigadoon
Color Magic
Double Delight
Graceland
Honor
Just Joey
Las Vegas
Midas Touch
Mikado
Mon Cheri
Olympiad
Pascali
Perfect Moment
Pristine
Rio Samba
Secret
Sheer Bliss

Floribundas
Amber Queen
Angel Face
Cathedral
Class Act
First Edition
First Kiss
French Lace
Iceberg
Playboy
Pleasure

Regensberg
Sexy Rexy
Showbiz
Sunflare
Sunsprite
Trumpeter

Grandifloras
Gold Medal
Love
Olé
Shining Hour
Tournament of Roses

Miniatures
Cupcake
Debut
Gourmet Popcorn
Holy Toledo
Little Artist
Magic Carrousel
Popcorn
Winsome

Climbers
Altissimo
Climbing Iceberg
Dortmund
Dublin Bay
Joseph's Coat
White Dawn

Shrubs
Bonica
Carefree Wonder
Fair Bianca
Mary Rose
Sally Holmes

Disease-Resistant Roses

Few roses are completely resistant to all diseases, and luckily, few climates tend to host all of them. The type of climate where you live—whether it is often rainy or often dry—greatly influences which diseases will be more likely to infect your roses. Rust is a problem in parts of the West, but rarely in the rest of the country. Black spot occurs in areas that receive summer rainfall. The exposure and amount of sun your garden receives are also strong influences. When located in partial shade, for example, many rose varieties are more susceptible to mildew.

The *1978 Rose Annual*, published by the American Rose Society, contains a list of the most overall disease-resistant rose varieties. Varieties are listed in descending order of resistance. The list was compiled by a panel of representatives from public rose gardens across the United States. Since the list was published, many new varieties with excellent disease resistance have been released. The list also does not include many excellent old garden roses, species and shrub roses, many of which are disease resistant. Use this list as a guide if diseases tend to be a problem in your region. However, keep in mind that disease resistance varies from area to area and from year to year. Also refer to the regional lists of adapted roses on pages 28 to 30.

(H) hybrid tea, (G) grandiflora, (F) floribunda, (S) shrub.

Queen Elizabeth (G)
Prominent (H)
Miss All-American Beauty (H)
Pristine (H)
Peace (H)
Tiffany (H)
Cathedral (H)
Fragrant Cloud (H)
Pascali (H)
Europeana (F)

'Peace' hybrid tea

Receiving mention were: Mister Lincoln (H), and Gene Boerner (F)

The *1990 Rose Annual* also included a list of disease resistant varieties that were not on the above list:

Aquarius (H)
Double Delight (H)
Gold Medal (G)
Mon Cheri (H)
Pink Parfait (H)
Sunsprite (F)
White Masterpiece (H)

'Prominent' grandiflora

Notable new disease-resistant roses include:

All That Jazz (S)
Carefree Wonder (S)
French Lace (F)
Honor (H)
Olympiad (H)
Touch of Class (H)

Fragrant Roses

Who can resist the alluring fragrance of a rose? Young or old, few can walk by a rose in the flush of full bloom without bending down to sample the scent.

The rose is remarkable in that quite a number of different aromas are produced by the flowers. Experts have identified about 25 distinct rose fragrances, which are

'Double Delight hybrid tea

closely linked to flower color. You can experience this by visiting a local rose garden to "stop and smell the roses." You'll discover spicy fragrances of clove and cinnamon, fruity aromas of citrus and apples and heady musky scents. Most familiar is the musky, classic tea fragrance of many red and pink roses, which can be traced to their Damask heritage. White and yellow roses are more likely to have fruity or spicy scents.

The time of day to smell a rose varies according to flower color. Roses in the red shades seem to be most powerful during midday heat. The scent of white and yellow roses is fleeting and best enjoyed in the morning hours.

Many species roses, shrub and old garden roses, described in the "Gallery of Roses," are also often blessed with highly fragrant flowers. Consider these for your fragrance garden.

(H) hybrid tea, (G) grandiflora, (F) floribunda, (C) climber, (M) miniature.

Amber Queen (F)
America (C)
Angel Face (F)

'Mister Lincoln' hybrid tea

'Iceberg' floribunda

Apricot Nectar (F)
Arizona (G)
Beauty Secret (M)
Broadway (H)
Center Gold (M)
Chrysler Imperial (H)*
Cinderella (M)
Double Delight (H)*
Fragrant Cloud (H)*
Fragrant Memory (H)
Friendship (H)
Golden Showers (C)
Gold Medal (G)
Granada (H)*
Intrigue (F)
Judy Garland (F)
Margaret Merrill (F)
Mister Lincoln (H)
Neon Lights (F)
Oklahoma (H)
Party Girl (M)
Perfume Delight (H)
Regensberg (F)
Rose Parade (F)
Royal Gold (C)
Royal Highness (H)
Saratoga (F)
Starglo (M)
Sundowner (G)
Sunsprite (F)*
Sutter's Gold (H)*
Sweet Surrender (H)
Tiffany (H) *
Tropicana (H)
Voodoo (H)
White Lightnin' (G)

*Winner of James
Alexander Gamble
Award for Fragrance.

Long-Lasting Cut Flowers

Almost every rose makes a fine cut flower, but some do last longer in a vase than others. Following a few simple tips will also extend the life and beauty of a cut rose. Heres how to make cut flowers last longer:

Cut roses late in the afternoon, using sharp pruning shears to make a clean cut. Don't crush the stems. For varieties with fewer than 35 to 40 petals, cut when buds are still tight, before the petals begin to unfold.

For many-petaled varieties, cut flowers *just as* the first petals unfold. After cutting, submerge flowers in lukewarm water for about 20 minutes. If some time has passed since flowers were first removed from the plant, recut the stems, removing about one inch, holding the stem under water as you make the cut. This minimizes the contact of the stem with air. After the roses are arranged in a vase, change the water and recut the flower stems daily to prolong their

'Voodoo' hybrid tea

'Mikado' hybrid tea

longevity. Adding a commercial cut flower preservative to the water also extends the life of the blooms.

The following is a list of the best long-stemmed hybrid teas (H) and grandifloras (G). Most old garden roses also make good cut flowers.

Chrysler Imperial (H)
Double Delight (H)
Duet (H)
First Prize (H)
Fragrant Cloud (H)
Granada (H)
Honor (H)
Mikado (H)
Miss All-American Beauty (H)

Mister Lincoln (H)
Olympiad (H)
Paradise (H)
Pascali (H)
Peace (H)
Prima Donna (G)
Pristine (H)
Queen Elizabeth (G)
Sonia (G)
Swarthmore (H)
Tiffany (H)
Touch of Class (H)
Tropicana (H)

Roses with Single Flowers

Roses with single flowers, five to nine petals, have a special beauty. Their flowers are open-faced and more dogwood-like in appearance than those of a classic hybrid tea. Usually they have bright yellow stamens in the centers of

'Pascali' hybrid tea

the flowers. Included in this list are some excellent old-fashioned, species and shrub roses, which tend to have attractive single flowers.

(H) hybrid tea, (G) grandiflora, (F) floribunda, (C) climber, (M) miniature, (OGR) old garden rose and species rose, (S) shrub.

Altissimo (C)
Betty Prior (F)
Dainty Bess (H)
Dortmund (C)

Eye Paint (F)
Golden Wings (S)
Meidiland (S)
Pink Meidiland (S)
Rosa bractata Mermaid
   (OGR)
Rosa eglanteria (OGR)
Rosa foetida bicolor (OGR)
Rosa hugonis (OGR
Rosa rugosa rosea (OGR)
Sally Holmes (S)
Simplex (M)
Starglo (M)

Roses for Hedges

Hedges are useful to define spaces or separate areas of the garden. Almost any floribunda rose makes a suitable hedge. They also make fine borders between fences and walkways and attractive backgrounds for other plants. In addition to flower color, the mature height and spread of a variety is the most important consideration when choosing hedge plants. Some old garden roses can grow quite large and will function as a screen or barrier as well as a hedge. Most of the floribundas are more restrained and easily kept 3 to 4 feet high.

To form a dense hedge, space floribundas 1 to 2 feet apart. Space more

'Camelot' grandiflora

vigorous roses 3 to 4 feet apart. Here are some of the most manageable roses for hedges.

(G) grandiflora, (F) floribunda, (OGR) old garden rose and species rose, (S) shrub.

All That Jazz (S)
Amber Queen (F)
Betty Prior (F)
Camelot (G)
Carefree Wonder (S)
Cathedral (F)
Cherish (F)
Class Act (F)
Europeana (F)
First Edition (F)
Gene Boerner (F)
Golden Wings (S)
Iceberg (F)
Playboy (F)
Pleasure (F)
Queen Elizabeth (G)
Rosa rugosa (OGR)
Sarabande (F)
Sexy Rexy (F)
Showbiz (F)
Simplicity (F)
Sparrieshoop (S)
Sunsprite (F)
Sweet Inspiration (F)
Trumpeter (F)

Roses for Edgings

Miniature roses are perfect for edging walkways, flower borders, and other plantings. Space plants 1 to 2 feet apart for a solid edging. Here are some of the best miniatures (M), plus a few polyanthas (P), to use as edgings.

Beauty Secret (P)
Center Gold (M)
Child's Play (M)
China Doll (P)
Cupcake (M)
Debut (M)
Figurine (M)
Gourmet Popcorn (M)
Judy Fischer (M)
New Beginnings (M)
Pride 'n' Joy (M)
Rise 'n' Shine (M)
Rosmarin (M)
Starglo (M)
Starina (M)
Yellow Doll (M)

'Carefree Wonder' shrub rose

Roses for Ground Covers

Many of the roses listed below are quite vigorous plants that are best used in large areas or on banks. These should be spaced 3 to 4 feet apart for a solid cover. The more restrained growers like 'Dortmund' and 'Sea Foam' can be planted slightly closer.

In addition to these varieties, many climbing and species roses can be used as ground covers if their canes are *pegged* to the ground. Some spreading floribundas, such 'Europeana', can also be planted in a mass to become effective ground covers.

(C) climber, (M) miniature, (P) polyantha, (OGR) old garden rose or species rose (S) shrub.

Alba Meidiland (S)
Dortmund (C)
New Dawn (C)
Pearl Meidiland (S)
Red Cascade (M)
Red Meidiland (S)
Repens Meidiland (S)
Rosa banksiae (OGR)
Rosa bracteata Mermaid
   (OGR)

Scarlet Meidiland (S)
Sea Foam (OGR)
The Fairy (P)
White Meidiland (S)

Roses by Color

Few flowers can match the color variety, intensity and richness of the rose. And, not surprisingly, for many gardeners, flower color is the most important criterion for selection. Rose flowers come in every shade except true blue and green. There are varieties, such as red 'Mister Lincoln', that possess

'Rise 'n' Shine' miniature

remarkable clarity in a single shade. Distinctly bicolored roses, such as red and white 'Double Delight', and colorful blended roses, such as yellow, orange and pink 'Joseph's Coat', offer additional and unique ways to enjoy the beauty of the rose.

It is often a surprise to many gardeners that the color of a rose can change with the weather or be a different shade from one region to another. Heat, humidity and amount of sunshine are some of the common climatic factors. For example, 'Granada' may be a beautiful mixture of pink and yellow tones during the cool, cloudy days of spring. With increasing sun and heat of summer, the deeper pink tones begin to predominate. Yellow roses are also more intensely colored in cloudy weather. Red roses are usually most deeply colored in hot, humid weather. More information on this subject can be found on page 12.

The best way to help ensure that a rose will be the color you want is to observe it growing locally. Visit a public rose garden in your area or view your neighbor's roses.

(H) hybrid tea, (G) grandiflora, (F) floribunda, (C) climber, (M) miniature, (P) polyantha, (OGR) old garden rose or shrub rose and (S) shrub.

Red Roses
Acey Deucy (M)
Altissimo (C)
American Spirit (H)
Beauty Secret (M)
Billie Teas (M)
Black Jade (M)
Blaze (C)

Carrousel (G)
Chrysler Imperial (H)
Debut (M)
Don Juan (C)
Dublin Bay (C)
Europeana (F)
Frensham (F)
Love (G)
Mikado (H)
Mister Lincoln (H)
Oklahoma (H)
Old Glory (M)
Olympiad (H)
Othello (S)
Precious Platinum (H)
Prospero (S)
Red Cascade (M)
Red Devil (H)
Red Meidiland (S)
Scarlet Meidiland (S)
Showbiz (F)
Starina (M)
Swarthmore (H)
Tempo (C)
Viva (F)

Pink Roses
All That Jazz (S)
America (C)
Aquarius (G)
Baby Betsy McCall (M)
Betty Prior (F)
Bonica (S)
Bridal Pink (F)
Carefree Wonder (S)
Cécile Brunner (F)
Cherish (F)
China Doll (P)
Cinderella (M)
Color Magic (H)
Cuddles (M)
Cupcake (M)
Dainty Bess (H)
David Thompson (S)
Duet (H)
First Kiss (F)
First Prize (H)
Fragrant Memory (H)
Friendship (H)
Funny Girl (M)
Gene Boerner (F)
Gertrude Jekyll (S)
Heritage (S)
The Fairy (P)
Judy Fischer (M)
Lilian Austin (S)
Mary Rose (S)
Miss All-American
Beauty (H)
Montezuma (G)
Morden Centennial (S)

Neon Lights (F)
New Dawn (C)
Origami (F)
Perfume Delight (H)
Pink Meidiland (S)
Pink Parfait (G)
Pleasure (F)
Prairie Dawn (S)
Prairie Princess (S)
Prima Donna (G)
Queen Elizabeth (G)
The Reeve (S)
Rose Parade (F)
Royal Highness (H)
Sea Pearl (F)
Seashell (H)
Sexy Rexy (F)
Sharifa Asma (S)
Sheer Elegance (H)
Simplicity (F)
Sonia (G)
Sparrieshoop (S)
Summer Dream (H)
Sweet Inspiration (F)
Sweet Surrender (H)
Tiffany (H)
Touch of Class (H)
Tournament of Roses (G)
Unforgettable (H)
Wife of Bath (S)
William Baffin (S)

Orange Roses
Apricot Nectar (F)
Brandy (H)
Brass Band (F)
Butterscotch (C)
Caribbean (G)
Cathedral (F)
Dolly Parton (H)
First Edition (F)
Fragrant Cloud (H)
Gingersnap (F)
Impatient (F)
Just Joey (H)
Kathy (M)
Margo Koster (P)
Marina (F)
Mary Marshall (M)
Medallion (H)
New Beginnings (M)
Olé (G)
Perdita (S)
Prominent (G)
Sally Holmes (S)
Sarabande (F)
Sheri Anne (M)
Sundowner (G)
Tropicana (H)
Trumpeter (F)

Yellow Roses
Abraham Darby (S)
Amber Queen (F)
Bojangles (M)
Cal Poly (M)
Center Gold (M)
Eclipse (H)
Golden Showers (C)
Gold Medal (G)
Golden Wings (S)
Graceland (H)
Graham Thomas (S)
King's Ransom (H)
Midas Touch (H)
Oregold (H)
Rise 'n' Shine (M)
Royal Gold (C)
Sequoia Gold (M)
Shining Hour (G)
Summer Sunshine (H)
Sun Flare (F)
Sunsprite (F)
Sutter's Gold (H)
Yellow Doll (M)

Lavender Roses
Angel Face (F)
Blue Girl (H)
Intrigue (F)
Lady X (H)
Lavender Jewel (M)
Paradise (H)
Royal Amethyst (H)
Spellcaster (G)
Winsome (M)

White Roses
Alba Meidiland (S)
Anastasia (H)
Class Act (F)
Cloud Nine (M)
Evening Star (F)
Fair Bianca (S)
Figurine (M)
French Lace (F)
Garden Party (H)
Gourmet Popcorn (M)
Honor (H)
Iceberg (F)
Ivory Fashion (F)
Ivory Tower (H)
John F. Kennedy (H)
Lace Cascade (C)
Margaret Merrill (F)
Pascali (H)
Pearl Meidiland (S)
Pristine (H)
Sea Foam (S)
Sheer Bliss (H)
Simplex (M)
Snow Bride (M)

Starglo (M)
White Dawn (C)
White Lightnin' (G)
White Masterpiece (H)
White Meidiland (S)

Multicolored Roses
Arizona (G)
Brigadoon (H)
Broadway (H)
Charisma (F)
Chicago Peace (H)
Child's Play (M)
Dortmund (C)
Double Delight (H)
Dreamglo (M)
Dynasty (H)
Eye Paint (F)
Granada (H)
Gypsy Carnival (F)
Handel (C)
Heavenly Days (M)
High Noon (C)
Holy Toledo (M)
Joseph's Coat (C)
Judy Garland (F)
Kathy Robinson (M)
Las Vegas (H)
Little Artist (M)
Little Darling (F)
Magic Carrousel (M)
Mon Cheri (H)
Nevada (S)
Over the Rainbow (M)
Party Girl (M)
Party Time (H)
Peace (H)
Peaches 'n' Cream (M)
Peppermint Twist (F)
Perfect Moment (H)
Pinata (C)
Playboy (F)
Prairie Flower (S)
Pride 'n' Joy (M)
Princesse de Monaco (H)
Puppy Love (M)
Rainbow's End (M)
Razzle Dazzle (F)
Redgold (F)
Regensberg (F)
Rio Samba (H)
Rosmarin (M)
Secret (H)
Shreveport (G)
Singin' in the Rain (F)
Sonia (G)
Toy Clown (M)
Voodoo (H)

Roses with the Highest ARS Ratings

The American Rose Society rating system is a good guide to selecting high-quality roses. The list following includes varieties described in this book that have been awarded a rating of 8.0 or higher. These roses are proven to be outstanding performers in gardens across the United States.

For information on how they are selected, see page 37. Keep in mind that ratings can change slightly year to year. The ratings listed here are from 1993. Newer varieties have not been in cultivation long enough to receive a rating.

Hybrid Teas
Red and orange
Fragrant Cloud (8.3)
Mister Lincoln (8.8)
Olympiad (9.1)
Swarthmore (8.1)

Pink
Beauty (8.2)
Color Magic (8.2)
Dainty Bess (8.3)
First Prize (8.9)
Miss All-American
   Beauty (8.2)
Royal Highness (8.2)
Tiffany (8.3)

White
Garden Party (8.2)
Pascali (8.1)
Pristine (9.2)

Mauve
Lady X (8.3)

Blend
Double Delight (8.9)
Paradise (8.3)
Peace (8.6)
Touch of Class (9.5)

Floribundas
Red and orange
Apricot Nectar (8.2)
Europeana (9.0)

Margo Koster (8.3)
Sarabande (8.0)
Showbiz (8.6)
Trumpeter (8.3)

Pink
Betty Prior (8.2)
Bridal Pink (8.4)
Cécile Brunner (8.1)
Cherish (8.3)
China Doll (8.3)
The Fairy (8.7)
Gene Boerner (8.5)
Sexy Rexy (9.0)
Simplicity (8.1)

White
Evening Star (8.2)
French Lace (8.2)
Iceberg (8.7)
Ivory Fashion (8.6)
Margaret Merrill (8.0)

Yellow
Sun Flare (8.1)
Sunsprite (8.7)

Mauve
Angel Face (8.1)

Blend
Eye Paint (8.1)
First Edition (8.6)
Little Darling (8.6)
Playboy (8.1)
Regensberg (8.5)

Grandifloras
Pink
Aquarius (8.0)
Pink Parfait (8.2)
Queen Elizabeth (9.0)
Tournament of Roses (8.0)

Yellow
Gold Medal (8.8)

Blend
Sonia (8.1)

Climbers
Red and orange
Altissimo (9.3)
Don Juan (8.2)
Dublin Bay (8.5)

Pink
America (8.8)

White
Climbing Iceberg (8.8)

Blend
Dortmund (9.1)
Handel (8.2)

Miniatures
Red and orange
Acey Deucy (8.3)
Beauty Secret (8.4)
Mary Marshall (8.0)
Starina (9.0)

Pink
Cinderella (8.0)
Cupcake (8.5)

Yellow
Rise 'n' Shine (9.1)

White
Gourmet Popcorn (8.4)
Simplex (8.2)
Snow Bride (9.3)

Mauve
Winsome (8.5)

Blend
Dreamglo (8.5)
Little Artist (8.5)
Magic Carrousel (9.0)
Over the Rainbow (8.3)
Party Girl (9.0)
Peaches 'n' Cream (8.4)
Rainbow's End (9.0)
Toy Clown (8.1)

Shrub Roses
Red and orange
Lilian Austin (9.4)
Prairie Princess (8.5)

Pink
Bonica (9.1)
Heritage (8.7)
Mary Rose (8.7)
Sparrieshoop (8.6)
William Baffin (9.4)

White
Sally Holmes (9.5)

Blend
Prairie Flower (8.6)

GALLERY OF ROSES

This chapter includes descriptions of more than 200 varieties and species of roses. Although this listing represents a small fraction of the more than 20,000 roses that are, or once were, available, these varieties and species are among the best roses you can grow. Roses included in this chapter have proven to be well adapted in North American gardens. Some, such as 'Peace' hybrid tea and 'Iceberg' floribunda, have maintained a standard of excellence for decades. Others, such as shrub roses 'Bonica' and Carefree Wonder', are recent introductions. They have been thoroughly evaluated and qualify as superior roses. Regional favorites are included in lists on pages 28 to 30.

The great majority of roses listed are widely available, either through mail-order sources or at retail garden centers. Exceptions occur with shrub, species and old garden roses. Some will be harder to find than modern varieties. Still, those included in this book are among the best and most readily available.

The Rose Descriptions

Each rose (again with the exception of species, shrub and old garden roses) is described in a standard format to make it easier for you to make your selections. Information includes the year it was introduced, its American Rose Society (ARS) rating, the year honored (if applicable) as an All-America Rose Selection (AARS), and detailed descriptions of flower, fragrance, plant form and foliage.

All-America Rose Selections—This system was set up by rose growers in 1938 to evaluate new introductions. For a period of two years, each new rose is grown in more than 25 strictly governed test gardens in the United States. They are judged *poor, fair, good, very good* or *excellent* in 15 categories ranging from bud and flower form to fragrance, growth habit, foliage, disease resistance and overall value. Roses receiving the highest scores are designated "AARS Award Winners."

ARS Ratings—This unique rating system, developed by the American Rose Society, is a valuable tool for selecting roses. Each year, society members from across the United States carefully evaluate new and old roses for growth habit, bloom characteristics, disease resistance and many other traits. Ratings and remarks are tabulated by region and published in the *American Rose Annual*. After five years of evaluation, new rose ratings are averaged and included in the annual's *Roses in Review*.

'Peace', a hybrid tea, is one of the world's most popular roses.

Above: 'Touch of Class' hybrid tea is a highly rated rose and an AARS winner.

Glossary of Rose Terms

Rose lovers have a language all their own, full of tongue-twisting terms and phrases. To a beginner, rose descriptions, including the ones in this book, may seem overdone with too much detail. But roses are so alluring and growing them is so rewarding that the beginner eventually becomes the expert. Then there is never enough information.

As your experience with roses grows, you'll realize that many factors influence the appearance of a blossom, as well as how it opens as a cut flower and how the plant performs in the landscape. You'll find that the number of petals determines a blossom's character and that the shine of leaves affects how the plant looks in the garden. That is why rose descriptions are detailed. If you need clarification of the terminology used throughout the book, refer to this glossary.

Basal cane. Vigorous new growth originating from, or just above, the bud union.

Bicolor. A flower with two distinct colors, often on either side of the petals.

Blend. A rose with two or more colors that are blended rather than being distinctly separate.

Blind shoot. A vigorous shoot that doesn't produce a flower.

Bud. An unopened flower, or another name for an eye.

Budded. A method of propagation in which an eye is inserted into the stem of another plant, usually a rootstock.

Bud union. A swollen part of the stem, usually near the soil surface, where the flowering variety joins the rootstock.

Cane. The main structural branches of a rose, originating at or just above the bud union.

Climber. Used to describe a large group of vigorous, stiff-caned roses. Not truly climbing plants, they usually require the support of a trellis or arbor or are tied to a wall.

Cupped blossom. Open-centered flower with stamens showing. Often occurs with single flowers or semidouble flowers.

Deadheading. Removing spent flowers before they are allowed to form hips.

Disbudding. Removing small flower buds from just below a blossom growing at the tip of a stem. Doing so channels energy into the flower above, making it bigger and stronger.

Double flower. Having 24 or more petals. *Very double* is a term often used to describe blossoms with more than 50 petals.

Eye. A small, dormant, vegetative bud occurring where a leaf meets a stem.

Floribunda. Free-blooming, shrubby roses with flowers borne in clusters. Excellent landscape plants ranging in height from 2 to 5 feet. Most are upright, but some are spreading.

Grandiflora. Vigorous-growing, shrubby roses reaching 6 to 8 feet high, although some are smaller in stature. Flowers usually smaller than those of hybrid teas, borne singly or in clusters.

Hardiness. The amount of winter cold (usually expressed in minimum temperatures) a plant can withstand without injury or death.

Heel-in. Temporarily covering the roots of a bareroot plant with soil or mulch to prevent drying.

High-centered. Classic hybrid tea flower form with the center petals extending higher than those around them.

Hip. The seed capsule of a rose. Develops after the flower has faded. Usually a bright orange to red color. Many persist on the plant through fall and into winter and are very ornamental. High in vitamin C content and often used in teas.

Hybrid tea. The most popular type of rose, loved for the perfection of flower form. Plants are generally upright, ranging from 3 to 6 feet high.

Lateral. Side growth originating laterally from a cane.

Leaf node. The point at which a leaf was or is attached to a stem. Where eyes originate.

Miniature. Small rose plants, generally reaching 1 to 2 feet high. Flowers born singly or in clusters, some with hybrid tea-like form.

Nonrecurrent bloom. Blooms once a season, usually in spring or early summer.

Recurrent bloom. Blooming frequently, usually for several cycles during the growing season.

Recurving. A petal that folds outward.

Reverse. The back side of a petal.

Rootstock. The plant that provides the root system for the flowering variety (scion), which is budded or grafted to it.

Semidouble. Blossoms having 12 to 24 petals.

Shrub rose. A broad class of roses, ranging in height and form. Many known for their hardiness and disease resistance.

Single. Blossoms having 5 to 12 petals.

Species rose. A plant of distinct botanical identity (can reproduce itself from seed with little variation) that can be found growing wild in its native area.

Sport. A naturally occurring mutation.

Stamens. The male reproductive parts of a flower, including the pollen. Usually bright yellow and often an attractive portion of a blossom.

Sucker. An undesirable shoot originating from below the bud union. It usually looks different from other canes on the plant and should be removed at its origin.

Tree rose. Not actually a type of rose, but a way of training rose varieties on a combination of rootstocks so they form a small, lollipop-like tree. They usually lack winter hardiness and need protection in most cold-winter climates.

Wild rose. A term often used to described species roses.

Mail-Order Roses

Mail-order catalogs offer the widest selection of both old and new roses. Most mail-order roses are grafted on vigorous rootstocks and sold bareroot. However, some nurseries have begun to sell plants grown on their own roots for increased hardiness as well as to ensure the roses are virus-free.

Here are some of the best mail-order rose sources. Prices for catalogs are subject to change. Some companies deduct the catalog cost from your order.

Antique Rose Emporium
Route 5, Box 143
Brenham, TX 77833
(800) 441-0002
Catalog: $5.
Colorful and informative catalog of heirloom and shrub roses, propagated on their own roots. Includes some "found" roses, varieties thought lost but recently propagated from plants found on old home sites or in cemeteries.

Edmund's Roses
6235 S.W. Kahle Road
Wilsonville, OR 97070
(503) 682-1476
Catalog: Free.
Well-respected growers offering modern roses in a neat color catalog. Varieties are artistically described.

Heirloom Old Garden Roses
24062 Riverside Dr., N.E.
Saint Paul, OR 97137
(503) 538-1576
Catalog: $5.
Huge selection of new and old roses grown on their own roots; many David Austin roses. Informative, colorful catalog. Plants shipped year-round.

High Country Rosarium
1717 Downing St.
Denver, CO 80218
(303) 832-4026
Catalog: Free.
Specializes in hardy old garden, shrub and species roses.

Hortico Inc.
723 Robson Rd.
Waterdown, ON, Canada LOR 2H1
(905) 689-6984
Catalog: $3.
Import catalog, carrying a huge selection of old and new roses, especially ones hard to find elsewhere.

Plants are smaller than those from most other nurseries, but are of high quality.

Jackson & Perkins
2518 South Pacific Highway
Medford, OR 97501
(800) 854-6200
Catalog: Free.
Color catalogs featuring roses, perennials, bulbs and gift items. Exclusive varieties. Includes helpful tips from garden experts.

Lowe's Own Root Rose Nursery
6 Sheffield Road
Nashua, NH 03062
(603) 888-2214
Catalog: $2.
Renowned specialist in own-root roses shipped October-November only. Huge selection, especially of hardy types. Delivery may take 18 months.

Nor'East Miniature Roses
PO Box 307
Rowley, MA 01969
(800) 426-6485
Catalog: Free.
Large selection of miniatures shipped year-round.

Pixie Treasures
4121 Prospect Ave.
Yorba Linda, CA 92686
(714) 993-6780
Catalog : $1.
Miniature rose specialist. More than 125 varieties available. Over 20,000 plants on display.

Roses of Yesterday and Today
802 Brown's Valley Road
Watsonville, CA 95076
(408) 724-3537
Catalog: $5.
Mails a wonderfully descriptive catalog of mostly old garden roses. Many rose growers consider it a collector's item.

Sequoia Nursery
2519 East Noble Ave.
Visalia, CA 93292
Catalog: Free.
Home nursery of renowned rose breeder Ralph Moore. Carries miniatures, shrubs and floribundas.

Tiny Petals
489 Minot Ave.
Chula Vista, CA 91910
(619) 422-0385
Catalog: Free.
Many varieties. Ships year-round.

Vintage Gardens
3003 Pleasant Hill Road
Sebastapol, CA 95472
(707) 829-5342
Catalog: $4.
Color catalog features an interesting mix of old garden roses. Availability list of "Antique and Extraordinary Roses" is free.

Wayside Gardens
PO Box 1
Hodges, SC 29695-0001
(800) 845-1124
Catalog: Free.
Offers wide range of plants, including old and new roses.

Natural Pest Controls

Several mail-order companies sell a wide range of botanical pesticides, insect predators and other alternative pest controls through informative catalogs. These following can get you started.

Gardens Alive!
5100 Schenly Place
Lawrenceburg, IN 47025
(812) 537-8650
Catalog: Free.

Necessary Trading Company
One Nature's Way
New Castle, VA 24127
(703) 864-5103
Catalog: Free.

Peaceful Valley Farm Supply
PO Box 2209
Grass Valley, CA 95945
(916) 272-4769
Catalog: Free.

Products & Services For Natural Agriculture
333 Ohme Gardens Road
Wenatchee, WA 98801
(800) 332-3179
Catalog: Free.

Irrigation Supplies
The Urban Farmer Store
2833 Vicente St.
San Francisco, CA 94116
(415) 661-2204
Catalog: $1.
Extensive catalog is an excellent source of information and supplies for drip irrigation.

Old Garden Roses and Shrub Roses

Old garden roses are the forerunners and parents of all modern roses. Some are distinct species, while others are groups of hybrids. Shrub roses comprise a diverse group of plants that offer great variety, character and versatility. They are not as simple to categorize as the modern and commonly used categories of hybrid tea, floribunda, grandiflora, miniature and climber. Roses in these classes are described later in this chapter. Shrub roses have recently enjoyed a surge of popularity with landscape gardeners, so much so that some rose nurseries are introducing groups of plants labeled as landscape shrub roses.

A fair number of the roses included in this section could actually be categorized as floribunda, shrub or miniature, depending on the variety. But because most are sold as landscape roses and are often grown on their own roots, rather than grafted to a rootstock, they are included here.

Right: 'Sally Holmes' is a functional and colorful cover. White rose at right is 'Madame Alfred Carrière'.

Opposite, top: David Austin English roses are becoming exceedingly popular as landscape roses. One of the best is yellow-flowering 'Graham Thomas'. In the background is light pink 'Cymbalene'.

Opposite, bottom left: Prairie rose, *Rosa setigera,* creates an interesting pattern with its single pink flowers and bright green, crinkly leaves.

Opposite, bottom right: Many old roses produce attractive rose *hips,* the fruit of the rose, which remain on the plant after flowers have passed. Shown is 'Frau Dagmar Hartopp', a *Rosa rugosa* hybrid.

Old Garden Roses

The rose family is an incredibly large one, comprising hundreds of species and thousands of hybrids. It includes plants that have been grown for centuries and have dramatically different appearances and growth habits compared to most modern hybrids. Many have rich histories, linked directly to colorful figures such as Napoleon and his wife Josephine and the early settlers of America. Others are blessed with distinctive beauty in fragrance, flower, foliage and fruit. These roses have often contributed their attributes as parents to today's modern hybrids.

Old garden roses have recently enjoyed a great surge in popularity. Species and varieties that were once rare and difficult to locate have become easier to find in specialty catalogs (see page 39). Most old garden roses are large, sturdy, easy-to-grow plants. If you need a tough yet attractive plant for a difficult situation, consider one of these roses. Many are long-lived landscape plants useful as hedges, screens and, if properly trained, colorful, low-maintenance ground covers. The graceful, informal and often sprawling habit of many old garden roses lends itself perfectly to a natural garden or old-style cottage garden.

In addition to attractive flowers, many produce colorful *hips*—the fruit of the rose—in fall and winter. Others have distinctive foliage that provides interest in the landscape during the entire growing season.

Old garden roses are some of the hardiest roses available, capable of withstanding the rigors of severe winters. You can also select vigorous plants adapted to grow in poor soils, and disease-resistant roses that do not require spraying. Most old garden roses also require little pruning, other than removing dead wood, or an occasional trimming to keep plants compact or within bounds.

Many old roses, such as teas, Chinas, Bourbons and hybrid perpetuals, are *repeat bloomers*, meaning they bloom more than once during the growing season. Others, such as Gallicas, bloom only in spring, but often for as long as six weeks. You can treat these seasonal bloomers as part of your perennial garden and integrate them into your garden's seasonal color scheme. This is discussed in more detail on page 20.

The following is a selection of the best old garden roses. For easy reference, some are organized by species, although the most available forms are usually hybrids between that species and other rose types. Specialty catalogs offer many more types as well as interesting information on culture, use and history.

Species Roses

Species roses, sometimes called *wild roses*, distinguish themselves from hybrids by growing true from seed when self-pollinated. As you look at this diverse group, you begin to get a true feeling for the great diversity of the rose family. Species roses can be found growing in the wild all the way from the arctic circle to the equator. Few plant genuses thrive under such a wide range of growing conditions.

Species roses tend to be vigorous, arching or sprawling plants that have one long bloom period in spring. If grown on their own roots, they tend to spread; if budded onto a different rootstock they generally remain in one place. Most have small flowers with five petals. Many have colorful hips, the rose fruit. Even though species roses have one blooming season, it is usually quite spectacular, with profuse numbers of flowers. The plants are well suited to naturalized landscapes and are commonly grown as sprawling shrubs or climbers. With a little pruning they can also be maintained as mounding shrubs or trained into trees or hedges.

Rosa banksiae

Lady Banks Rose

This sprawling, thornless rose produces large clusters of small, fragrant, yellow or white flowers in late spring. It remains evergreen in mild climates. Lady Banks rose is long-lived but is more tender to cold than most roses, surviving temperatures to about 15F.

Plants grow vigorously and can easily spread to 20 feet. They are attractive when allowed to climb on large, sturdy supports such as trellises, fences or arbors. They also make excellent mounding ground covers. *Rosa banksiae* 'Alba Plena' has sweetly fragrant, double white flowers. *R. b.* 'Lutea' has double yellow flowers.

Rosa bracteata

'Mermaid'

Light yellow, single flowers are borne on a vigorous, climbing plant that can reach 30 feet or more high. Flowers appear all season. Leaves are glossy deep green and remain evergreen in mild climates. Does well in the toughest locations, even in shade. Disease resistant. Use as a ground cover or train on arbors or tall fences. Also works well as a natural fence.

Rosa eglanteria

Sweetbrier, Eglantine Rose

A vigorous, arching, spring-blooming shrub that produces small, soft pink, single flowers in clusters. Foliage and flowers have an apple-like fragrance. Leaves are dark green and slightly rough. They emit their fragrance when weather is windy or rainy. Hips are reddish orange. Can be planted as a hedge or security screen. A natural candidate for fragrance gardens.

Rosa foetida bicolor

Austrian Copper Rose

A hardy, spring-blooming shrub that reaches 4 to 5 feet high. Single flowers are bright scarlet-orange with yellow reverse. Tends to get black spot disease.

Rosa x harisonii

Harison's Yellow Rose

A tough, hardy, disease-resistant and drought-tolerant deciduous shrub. Bright yellow, semidouble flowers are fragrant and bloom in spring. Attractive, rich green foliage covers the spreading plant, which can grow to 6 feet high.

Rosa hugonis

Father Hugo Rose

Produces sprays of single, light yellow flowers in spring. Blossoms are borne on arching stems, reaching 6 to 8 feet high, covered with handsome, fernlike, deep green leaves. Useful on a trellis, on a fence or as a screen. Extremely hardy.

Rosa roxburghii

Chestnut Rose

An unusual species with buds that open into pink, lightly fragrant flowers. Flowers open intermittently throughout the growing season. They are followed by bristly hips that resemble chestnuts, the inspiration for the flower's common name. Leaves are finely divided, with a light-textured appearance. Plants reach 5 to 7 feet high but are easily kept smaller with pruning. Interesting bark. Hardy to about 0F. See photo page 8.

■ ■ ■

Old Garden Roses in the Rocky Mountains

Intense sunlight, heavy snow and bitterly cold winters makes growing roses at high elevation a challenge. For help, order a catalog from High Country Rosarium (see page 39 for address). They specialize in high-elevation roses. Their informative catalog includes lists of roses to attract birds, drought-tolerant roses and special roses that are adapted to grow above 6,000 feet elevation.

■ ■ ■

Right: Lady Banks rose, *Rosa banksiae,* a species rose, has a sprawling growth habit, producing small, fragrant flowers in spring. It remains evergreen in mild-climate regions.

Far right: Harison's yellow rose, *Rosa x harisonii,* is tough, hardy, disease resistant and drought-tolerant. Bright yellow, semidouble flowers are fragrant and bloom in spring. Attractive, rich green foliage covers the spreading plant, which can grow to 6 feet high.

Below: 'Boule de Neige', a Bourbon rose, produces clusters of fragrant white flowers from midsummer to fall.

Below right: *Rosa foetida bicolor,* Austrian copper rose, is a hardy, spring-blooming shrub that reaches 4 to 5 feet high. Single flowers are bright scarlet-orange with yellow reverse.

Left: 'Zéphirine Drouhin', a Bourbon rose, can be grown as a small shrub or climber. Magenta-pink flowers bloom during summer into fall. Rose on wall in the background is 'Fortune's Double Yellow'.

Below left: Portland rose 'Jacques Cartier' grows to about 3-1/2 feet high. Flowers have a sweet fragrance.

Below: In addition to attractive flowers, the rugosa 'Belle Poitevine' has colorful fall foliage and hips.

Gallery of Roses: Old Garden Roses and Shrub Roses ■ 45

Rosa setigera

Prairie Rose

This is a delightful rambler native to North America. It produces small, single
pink flowers, mainly in spring that are followed by red hips. Plants have a
sprawling growth habit and can be used as a shrub or climber.

Other Old Garden Roses

Here are the major groupings of old garden roses. They are grouped by common
parents or similar heritage.

Alba Roses

The albas you purchase today are probably hybrids between the dog rose, *Rosa
canina*, and Damask roses. They are useful, upright-growing plants that reach
about 6 feet high. They are extremely disease resistant, with healthy, robust,
finely toothed, blue-green leaves. Albas grow well in poor soils and are better
adapted to partially shaded areas than many roses. Stems are nearly thornless
and most plants are hardy to cold. Albas bloom for a long period in spring. The
flowers are sweetly fragrant in shades of white and pink.

Varieties include 'Königin von Dänemark', with multipetaled, light pink flowers.
'Félicité Parmentier' has white flowers with pink centers. 'Madame Plantier' is a
beautiful plant with double white flowers.

Bourbon Roses

These roses are named for an island off Madagascar where the original natural
hybrid was discovered. Bourbon roses are historically important as contributors
of red color in the development of many hybrid teas. Most are compact,
vigorous, shrublike plants or restrained climbers. Leaves are an attractive shiny
green. Flower colors are mainly shades of pink and red, blooming primarily in
spring but with intermittent repeat blooms throughout the year. Plants are hardy
to about 0F degrees, and are subject to black spot.

Several varieties are available, including light pink and wonderfully fragrant
'Souvenir de la Malmaison,' and the highly fragrant pinks 'Madame Isaac
Pereire' and 'Madame Ernst Calvat'. 'Madame Isaac Pereire' is excellent when
trained on a low fence. 'Boule de Neige' is an attractive shrub with fragrant white
flowers. 'Louise Odier' has stunning camellia-like pink flowers. It is a good
repeat bloomer with intense fragrance. 'Honorine de Brabant' is a repeat-
blooming, bicolored Bourbon with light pink flowers striped with crimson and
purple. The blossoms have a strong raspberry scent. A vigorous plant, it can be
grown as a tall shrub or a climber. 'La Reine Victoria' has sweetly fragrant, rich
pink cupped flowers on an upright plant.

Rosa centifolia

Cabbage Roses

These are compact-to-large, shrubby roses, with a single but spectacular bloom
period in spring. Pink to purple flowers bloom in late spring and early summer,
emitting a pleasant, spicy fragrance. Flowers are made up of thin, overlapping
petals, hence their common name. 'Fantin-Latour' (sometimes listed as a hybrid
China) and 'Tour de Malakoff' are two pink-flowering varieties. 'Rose de Meaux'
is a small plant, miniaturelike in character, rarely reaching over 3 feet high. Its
small pink flowers are very fragrant. 'Zéphirine Drouhin' is a vigorous climber
with fragrant pink flowers that bloom over a long season.

Moss Roses

Moss roses are *sports*—naturally occurring mutations—of centifolias and Damasks.
They are named for the mossy looking, pine-scented hairs on their stems and

bases of the flowers. Today, however, "moss rose" has come to refer to any variety with hairy stems, including many damask roses. Moss roses were popular in Victorian times, loved for their intensely fragrant double flowers in shades of white, pink and red. Most are repeat bloomers. 'Alfred de Dalmas' is one of the better repeat-blooming moss roses. It has pink flowers that fade to white. Plants are compact and make an attractive hedge. 'Maréchal Davoust' blooms only once a season but has richly fragrant carmine pink flowers that darken to lilac purple.

China Roses

China roses are historically important shrub roses, contributing their everblooming character to a number of modern roses. Varieties such as 'Minima' are small plants and are parents of modern miniature roses. They are excellent used in pots, as edgings, for hedges or in small gardens. Plants are long-lived, disease resistant and hardy to about 0F. Most produce single flowers in clusters, but double forms are also available.

Popular China roses include 'Old Blush', which is also sold under the name 'Parsons' Pink China'. It has double pink flowers that are borne on a compact, dainty plant. This rose can truly be considered a low-maintenance flowering shrub. 'Hermosa' has nicely shaped, double, pink, fragrant blooms on a neat, compact plant. 'Archduke Charles' bears beautiful crimson blooms that lighten as the flower ages.

Rosa x noisettiana

Noisette Roses

Some noisettes are climbing forms; others are smaller plants grown as shrubs. They are best grown on a pillar or arbor or trained along a fence. Most produce fragrant flowers in shades of white, cream and yellow, and, on rare occasion, in red. Noisette roses have historical importance because they are responsible for contributing yellow and orange shades to many climbing roses. Most are not cold hardy and are damaged if temperatures drop much below freezing.

Varieties of noisette roses include white-flowering 'Jeanne d'Arc', which produces red hips. 'Fellemberg', sometimes listed as a China, is a cascading plant with crimson blooms. The intensely fragrant 'Madame Alfred Carrière' has hybrid tea-like, cream flowers. 'Alister Stella Gray' produces yellow flowers that fade to cream. The latter two also produce a colorful display of hips in fall.

Portland Roses

Portland roses are a blend of China, Damask and Gallica heritage. They were developed by a 19th-century hybridizer as repeat-blooming roses. However, after hybrid perpetuals and China roses increased in popularity, the Portlands lost favor. Plants are compact with very fragrant, double flowers. Few are available today. With some effort, you may find pink-flowering 'Jacques Cartier', 'Comte de Chambord' or red 'Rose du Roi'. 'Rose de Rescht' bears deep red blooms tinged with purple. They may have up to 100 petals and are wonderfully fragrant. The dense, compact plant is a good repeat bloomer.

Rosa rugosa

Rugosa Roses

This is an important species rose that helped produce many excellent hybrids. Most are extremely tough and hardy plants, with crinkly, deep green leaves and bright red hips. Plants normally reach 4 to 8 feet high and make excellent hedges. Plants tend to sucker profusely. Flowers are single to double and come in shades of white, pink to deep reddish purple and yellow. They produce a rich clove scent. Many varieties bloom both spring and fall and have brightly colored hips.

■ ■ ■

Pegging Old Roses for More Flowers

Pegging is a old-fashioned method of keeping many vigorous old garden roses and shrubs in bounds while increasing bloom. Select the most vigorous canes and secure them about 12 inches above the ground with stakes and wire. Cut the end of the cane back to two to three buds. Side shoots along the length of the cane will grow and bloom. In winter, shorten these shoots to two or three buds, as you would when training a climber. Many Bourbons and hybrid perpetuals bloom wonderfully when pegged.

■ ■ ■

Above: Rugosa hybrid 'Sarah Van Fleet' produces large, semidouble pink flowers.

Right: 'F. J. Grootendorst', ruffled, double, deep red flowers combines with light pink 'Grootendorst'.

Below: 'Fellemberg', a pink China rose, and the noisette rose 'Alister Stella Gray, with yellow flowers that fade to cream.

Favorite rugosa hybrids include 'F. J. Grootendorst', ruffled, double, deep red flowers; 'Hansa', with large, reddish purple flowers having intense spicy fragrance; *Rosa rugosa rosea*, single pink flowers; 'Belle Poitevine' has large double magenta-pink blooms; and 'Sarah Van Fleet', large, semidouble pink blooms. 'Sir Thomas Lipton' has double to semidouble white blossoms that have an intense fragrance.

Scotch Roses and Hybrid Pimpinellifolia

You can select from many varieties of these hardy, deciduous shrubs. Most have prickly stems. Springtime flowers range from white to pink and yellow; most are single. Many have attractive, ferny or crinkly foliage and bright red hips.

Some of the best selections include the 'Frühlings' series developed by Kordes. Look for yellow-flowering 'Frühlingsgold' and pink-flowering 'Frühlings-morgen'. 'Stanwell Perpetual' is a high-quality repeat-blooming rose with blush pink flowers.

Rosa damascena

Damask Rose

This is one of the oldest groups of roses, known for its intensely fragrant flowers borne in tight clusters. Blossoms come in shades of white, pink and red and are borne on thorny shrubs that reach about 6 feet high. Most are not repeat bloomers.

The variety called 'Autumn Damask' is a repeat-blooming pink rose. 'York and Lancaster' is an unusual variety whose flowers have some pink petals and some white petals. 'Léda', which is often called *painted Damask,* has very double, white flowers, with outer petals touched in pinkish red. 'Madame Hardy' is a gorgeous variety with clean white, cupped flowers that have an interesting green eye. Blooms have a lemon scent and cascade from arching canes. 'Marie Louise' bears an abundance of rich pink blooms on a lower-growing plant.

The apothecary's rose, *Rosa gallica officinalis,* is one of the oldest roses in cultivation, dating to the Crusades. The semidouble flowers hold their fragrance even when dried.

Rosa gallica

Gallicas, French Roses

These are often-hybridized spring-blooming roses with intensely fragrant flowers in shades of red, pink and purple. Sometimes flowers are mottled or multicolored. Golden yellow stamens are showy, as are the bright red hips. Another interesting feature is the foliage, which turns red in fall. Plants are upright and well behaved, spreading 3 to 4 feet wide.

The apothecary's rose, usually sold as *R.g. officinalis,* is one of the oldest roses in cultivation. It is important from a historical standpoint, dating back to the Crusades and said to have come to America with the Pilgrims. The light crimson flowers have a remarkable ability to hold their fragrance when dried. Consequently, they were widely used for medicinal purposes or to freshen homes. The plant grows as an upright bush form, reaching at least 4 feet high. Flowers, which bloom only in spring, are followed by bright red hips.

Among the varieties still available are 'Charles de Mills', which produces multi-petaled flowers in varying shades of red to purple. 'Camaieux' bears rosy purple flowers with white stripes. 'Empress Josephine' has pink flowers with ruffled petals veined in deeper pink.

Hybrid Perpetuals

These old roses were popular in the 19th century before modern hybrid teas captured the attention of rose growers. They have a complex heritage, with origins primarily in tea roses, Bourbons and Portlands. Flowers of hybrid perpetuals typically come in shades of pink, red, purple and sometimes white. Plants are vigorous, often with arching, climberlike canes. Flowers are usually multipetaled, and they bloom profusely in spring, although some bloom sporadically in summer or fall. They are fragrant and wonderful in bouquets.

Hybrid perpetuals currently available include pink-flowering 'Baronne Prévost', 'Baroness Rothschild', 'Paul Neyron', 'Georg Arends' and 'Heinrich Munch'. Those with red flowers include 'Henry Nevard' and 'Hugh Dickson'. Flowers in shades of purple can be found in 'Reine des Violettes'. The best white-flowering variety is 'Frau Karl Druschki'. 'Ferdinand Pichard' has pink- and scarlet-striped flowers. 'Vick's Caprice' is an interesting rose with lavender-pink blooms flecked and striped with white and dark pink.

Tea Roses

Another group of roses that have contributed greatly to the development of modern hybrids are the tea roses. The original tea roses were hybrids between the China rose and *Rosa gigantea.* Their heritage of pointed buds and ever-blooming flowers in shades of cream, pink and yellow are evident in many of today's hybrid teas. Plants are good repeat bloomers. Be aware they are relatively cold-tender.

Tea roses available today include the pink-flowering 'Catherine Mermet', 'Rosette Delizy', yellow flowers blushed red, and 'Sombreuil', a climbing rose with creamy white flowers. 'Lady Hillingdon' has deep apricot yellow flowers. 'Duchesse de Brabant' bears very fragrant, light rosy pink flowers on a vigorous, spreading plant. 'Eugène de Beauharnais' bears large, wonderfully fragrant, purple flowers.

Hybrid Musks

These roses are distantly linked to the musk rose, *Rosa moschata,* plus a blend of various other species. The flowers have the intense, musky, old rose aroma and are usually borne in large clusters. Many are good repeat bloomers: some have bright orange hips. Plants are vigorous shrubs with attractive, dark green leaves.

Popular hybrid musks include pink-flowering 'Felicia', yellow-flowering 'Penelope', and the beautiful, clear pink, single-flowered 'Ballerina'. 'Vanity' bears huge clusters of wonderfully fragrant, single, deep pink flowers. 'Lavender Lassie' bears large clusters of double, lavender-pink blossoms. It can be trained as a climber. 'Nymphenburg' is a large shrub with glossy, deep green leaves and soft salmon-pink flowers touched with yellow at the base. The blooms smell of apples and are followed by orange hips. 'Cornelia' has pink blooms with bright yellow stamens borne in flat sprays. It makes a nice hedge.

Shrub Roses

Most of the varieties of shrub roses described in the following were developed within the last 50 years. However, since the late 1980s there has been a surge of new landscape shrub rose releases, highlighted by the Meidiland roses, the David Austin English roses and varieties like 'Carefree Wonder' and 'All That Jazz', both honored as All-America Rose Selections. In addition, some nurseries now label selected varieties as "landscape roses," including the 'Simplicity' roses, which have long been categorized as floribundas, as they are in this book.

When considering roses for landscape situations, it is important not to focus solely on the newer shrub roses, although they are undeniably fine plants. Floribundas like 'Iceberg' and polyanthas such as 'China Doll' are proven landscape subjects. This is especially true of 'Iceberg', which is often used by rose breeders as one parent when hybridizing new shrub varieties.

Meidiland Roses

Meidiland roses were developed in Europe, and are grown and distributed in the United States by several nurseries. They are vigorous, hardy plants that are best located in large, expansive gardens or used as background or ground covers in more natural landscapes. Give them room to grow, spacing plants 3 to 4 feet apart. They are disease resistant and low maintenance, requiring little or no pruning. Most Meidiland roses cover themselves with huge clusters of flowers and are repeat bloomers. Some have brightly colored hips.

'Alba Meidiland'. Vigorous and spreading plant, growing 2 to 3 feet high and twice as wide. Small white flowers are borne throughout summer. Use as a ground cover or on slopes.

'Bonica'. Upright plant with arching stems that reach 2 to 4 feet high; slightly wider than tall. Large clusters of medium pink, double flowers bloom through-out summer. Bright red hips in fall. With light pruning, can be used as a hedge, or planted en masse, in borders or as a barrier. AARS 1987.

'Pearl Meidiland'. Vigorous, spreading plant, reaching 2 to 3 feet high and twice as wide. Medium-sized, double, white flowers with yellow centers. Use as a ground cover or on slopes.

'Pink Meidiland'. Vigorous, upright plant, 2 to 4 feet high and 2 to 3 feet wide. Large, single, pink flowers with white centers. Orange hips. Use as a hedge, in mass plantings or in containers.

'Red Meidiland'. Vigorous, spreading plant, growing 1 to 2 feet high and 5 to 6 feet wide. Large, single, red flowers with white centers. Red hips. Use as a ground cover.

'Scarlet Meidiland'. Vigorous, mounding plant 3 to 4 feet high and 5 to 6 feet wide. Small, deep red, double flowers in large clusters. Use as a large-scale ground cover or on slopes.

'White Meidiland'. Vigorous, spreading plant, reaching 1 to 2 feet high and 4 to 5 feet wide. Medium-sized, double white flowers. Disease resistant. Use as a ground cover.

■ ■ ■

Natural Garden Tip

When using insecticidal soaps, spray the entire plant thoroughly and repeat applications frequently. You may have to spray every few days until pest is under control. Apply in the morning or late afternoon to reduce evaporation. Read and follow all product label directions. Soaps can burn some plants and are most effective when mixed with soft water.

■ ■ ■

Right: Hybrid perpetual 'Ferdinand Pichard' flowers from midsummer into fall.

Far right: Hybrid perpetual 'Vick's Caprice' produces attractive pink-and-white striped flowers.

Below: Hybrid musk 'Lavender Lassie' is a handsome rose, trained here on an archway.

Opposite, top left: 'Lilian Austin' (orange-pink) and 'Gertrude Jekyll' (pink), two David Austin English roses, work well in combination.

Opposite, top right: 'Golden Wings' is a hardy repeat-blooming rose, producing long-lasting, attractive sulfur-yellow flowers.

Opposite, center right: David Austin rose 'Mary Rose' produces medium pink, fully double flowers with wonderful Damask fragrance. Free-branching, vigorous bush with an upright habit.

Opposite, bottom left: David Austin roses are available in a range of growth habits, from upright to sprawling. White rose in center is 'Perdita'.

Opposite, bottom right: 'Wise Portia' is a highly fragrant David Austin rose.

David Austin English Roses

These shrub roses were developed by English rose breeder David Austin. They combine the elegance of old rose flowers and fragrance with the repeat bloom of modern roses, particularly floribundas.

David Austin roses vary quite a bit in size and habit. Many are quite vigorous, reaching well over 6 feet high in one growing season. Consequently, they are best used in large borders, grouped in masses or pruned regularly during the growing season. They can also be trained along a fence; bending the canes increases the bloom on laterals. Other David Austins are more compact and are well suited to smaller gardens or containers. Relatively new to North America, they are unproven in many regions. In some climates they are prone to black spot and do not rebloom. However, they do offer the rose grower flowers and growth habits that are different from the usual rose forms. Following are some of the more common and reliable varieties.

'Abraham Darby'. Cupped, apricot yellow blooms are borne singly and in clusters on arching stems. Fruity fragrance. Tends to be very vigorous and not heavily foliaged. Best trained along a low fence.

'Fair Bianca'. Beautifully cupped blooms are white to yellow with green centers. Very fragrant. Small, light green leaves on a restrained plant, reaching 3 to 4 feet high. Suited to smaller gardens.

'Gertrude Jekyll'. Large, fully formed, glowing pink flowers swirl open to 4 inches across. Strong Damask fragrance. Vigorous, upright plant with dark green leaves. Grows 6 to 12 feet high. Blooms heaviest in spring. Cut back after the first bloom to encourage more flowers.

'Graham Thomas'. One of the most popular varieties. Apricot buds open into beautiful, clear yellow, cup-shaped blooms with tea rose fragrance. The plant is upright, reaching 8 to 12 feet high, with glossy, light green foliage. May need supports. Tends to bloom heaviest in spring.

'Heritage'. Large sprays of cupped, shell pink blossoms with intense, old rose fragrance touched with a hint of lemon. A strong, robust plant to 5 or 6 feet high. Canes have few thorns and clean-looking foliage.

'Lilian Austin'. Small clusters of fragrant, orange-pink, cupped blossoms. Low, spreading plant to about 3 feet high. Leaves are attractive dark green.

'Mary Rose'. Medium pink, fully double flowers with wonderful Damask fragrance. Free-branching, vigorous bush with an upright habit. Tends to mildew in humid climates.

'Othello'. Large, full-petaled, dark crimson flowers open beautifully, gradually turning to shades of purple and mauve. Vigorous, bushy plant reaches at least 4 to 6 feet high, with strong, stiff canes. Works well trained to a post or fence.

'Perdita'. Blush apricot blooms with intense, award-winning, tea fragrance are born in small clusters. Small, light green leaves on a rounded plant. Grows to about 3 feet high.

'Prospero'. Large sprays of heavily petaled, dark red flowers that resemble a gallica rose. Excellent rebloomer. Bright green foliage on a restrained, easy-to-care-for plant. Requires little pruning. Exceptional in warm-climate regions.

'Sharifa Asma'. A light pink rose with strong fragrance. Free-blooming, compact plant reaching about 3 feet high and as wide. Good in mild-winter climates.

'The Reeve'. Deep pink, cup-shaped flowers with intense, old-rose fragrance. Spreading, arching growth up to 4 feet high with dark, rough-textured leaves.

'Wife of Bath'. A small, free-blooming pink rose with the fragrance of myrrh. Grows as a compact, bushy plant, reaching about 4 feet high and 3 feet wide. Good in mild-winter climates.

'Wise Portia'. A magenta rose, reaching to 3 feet or more high. Strong fragrance.

Other Shrub Roses

'All That Jazz'. This lovely plant was a All-America Rose Selection in 1992. Large, salmon-orange blooms have 12 petals, bright yellow stamens in the center and a slight Damask fragrance. Flowers are produced throughout the season. The plant grows about 5 feet high and as wide. The attractive, disease-resistant foliage is dark, glossy green. Handsome when used as a hedge or border plant.

'Carefree Wonder'. All-America Rose Selection in 1991. A free-blooming plant yielding generous rich pink blossoms with creamy pink reverse. Grows 4 to 6 feet high with a rounded habit. Ideal border or hedge plant. Very disease resistant.

'Golden Wings'. A valuable shrub rose that produces early, long-lasting, large, single, sulfur-yellow flowers. Plants reach 4 to 6 high, are hardy and good repeat bloomers. Prone to black spot. Makes a fine hedge.

'Nevada'. Striking single white to pinkish blooms are marked with red on backs of petals. It blooms spring and fall, growing 6 to 8 feet high. Prone to black spot.

'Sally Holmes'. Clusters of apricot buds open into large, single white flowers. Light fragrance. Dark, glossy green foliage on a spreading, vigorous shrub.

'Sea Foam'. A vigorous, spreading rose that has become popular as a ground cover. Flowers "hang their heads," so one of the best locations is on a slope that one views from below. Double, creamy white flowers are borne in spring and fall. Handsome, deep green foliage.

'Sparrieshoop'. This is a bulky, upright plant that reaches 6 to 8 feet high. Wonderfully fragrant, single pink flowers are borne in spring and fall. Attractive, deep green, leathery leaves. Disease resistant and cold hardy. Useful as a hedge.

Cold-Hardy Shrub Roses

Several rose-breeding programs in the Midwest and Canada have produced shrub roses bred specifically for hardiness, pest resistance and abundant bloom. The following are excellent choices for cold-winter climates.

'Champlain'. Generous producer of dark red flowers from early summer to fall. Lightly fragrant. Compact shrub form, grows 3 feet high spreading 3 feet wide, with small green leaves. Resistant to mildew.

'David Thompson'. Fragrant, deep pink flowers borne in large clusters. Compact, rounded habit to about 3 feet high. Resists mildew and black spot.

'Morden Centennial'. One of the Parkland series of hardy roses from Canada. The pink, fragrant blossoms are borne in large clusters. Vigorous plant reaching 5 feet high and as wide. Flowers are produced on new wood so plants can be pruned heavily without reducing bloom. Resists mildew, black spot and rust.

'Prairie Dawn'. One of the Prairie series of hardy roses. Bright pink flowers on an upright plant reach 5 feet high. Good repeat bloom and disease resistance.

'Prairie Flower'. Single red flowers with white centers. Old-rose fragrance. Repeat bloomer. Upright, bushy growth. Leathery green leaves. Disease resistant.

'Prairie Princess'. Large, semidouble, coral-pink blooms with slight fragrance. Vigorous upright growth. Large, leathery, dark green leaves are disease resistant.

'William Baffin'. Deep pink, fragrant blossoms borne in large clusters. Vigorous plant growing 6 to 9 feet high. Can be treated as a climber or sprawling shrub. Requires little pruning or cold protection. Resistant to mildew and black spot.

Hybrid Teas

Hybrid teas are the most loved and widely grown of all roses. The reason is obvious: they are simply among the most beautiful flowers in the world. Their colors are clear and bright, seen in almost every shade except green and true blue. Flower form is exquisite, with elegant buds slowly swirling open into perfect, high-centered blossoms borne on strong, sturdy stems. They are unmatched as cut flowers. And what flower can surpass the fragrance of a hybrid tea? From musky to fruity to spicy, each variety has its own pleasing, characteristic scent.

In the 1940s, 'Peace' became a symbol of hope for the future. In the 1960s, 'Royal Highness' and 'Mister Lincoln' were the flowers of the decade. In the 1970s, the pink rose 'First Prize' set a new standard for perfection in flower form; 'Double Delight' became a favorite due to its outstanding color and substance. In the 1980s, 'Touch of Class' gained similar popularity. And, in the 1990s, varieties such as 'Secret' and Brigadoon' take center stage.

Here are the finest hybrid tea roses. Plants range in size from 3 to 6 feet high. Most are vigorous and upright, but a few, as noted in the descriptions, have a spreading growth habit.

'Double Delight' is a delight, with its striking, clean white blossoms tipped with strawberry red. This and the flower's alluring fragrance make it one of the most popular hybrid teas of the last 20 years.

Orange-red 'Mikado' and pink 'Prima Donna', a grandiflora, serve as colorful background plants for perennials and miniature roses.

The glowing yellow flowers of 'Graceland' are striking in combination with the red and yellow shades of 'Perfect Moment'.

American Spirit

ARS 7.4 Introduced 1988

A beautiful, velvety red rose borne on strong, sturdy stems. Blooms continuously through the season. Good cut flower.

Flower and Fragrance
Long, pointed, deep red buds spiral open into deep red blooms. Double, 5 inches, with 30 to 35 petals. Moderate fragrance.

Form and Foliage
Vigorous upright plant with dark green foliage. Tends to mildew in some areas. Quite hardy.

Anastasia

ARS 7.2 Introduced 1980

A clear white rose with exceptional flower form. Long-lasting on the plant and in the vase. Easy to grow and widely adapted.

Flower and Fragrance
Shapely, pointed buds open into classic, high-centered, white blooms. Double, 3 to 4 inches, with 30 petals. Little fragrance.

Form and Foliage
Vigorous upright plant with dark green leaves. Good disease resistance.

Blue Girl

ARS 5.6 Introduced 1965

An unusual silvery lavender hybrid tea sold as a blue rose. Prolific bloomer.

Flower and Fragrance
Nicely shaped lavender buds open into large, silvery lavender-blue flowers. Double, 5-1/2 inches, with 30 to 35 petals. Light, fruity fragrance.

Form and Foliage
Medium-sized bushy plant with good vigor. Medium green foliage.

Brandy

ARS 7.3 Introduced 1982, AARS 1982

A rich blend of apricot-colored hues with a wonderful, fruity fragrance. Requires winter protection in coldest climates.

Flower and Fragrance
Apricot-orange buds open quickly into loose open blossoms in warm shades of apricot-orange. Double, 4 to 4-1/2 inches, with 25 to 30 petals. Slight tea fragrance.

Form and Foliage
Vigorous and upright plant with semiglossy green leaves.

Brigadoon

ARS ___ Introduced 1991, AARS 1992

A tall, upright hybrid tea with rich blends of coral pink. Widely adapted with very good disease resistance. Long-stemmed cut flower. Combines beautifully with other pink, white and blue flowers.

Flower and Fragrance
Long, pointed, ovoid buds open into coral pink blooms, lighter at the base and with cream reverse. Double, 5-1/2 inches, with 25 to 30 petals. Light fragrance.

Form and Foliage
Tall, upright plant with deep green leaves. Very good disease resistance.

Broadway

ARS 6.5 Introduced 1986, AARS 1987

Brightly colored orange-rose suffused with gold and pink tones. Prolific producer of fragrant blooms. Best color when grown in cool-summer climates.

Flower and Fragrance
Large, multicolored buds open into orange blossoms blended with red and yellow at the base of the outer petals. Double, 3-1/2 to 4-1/2 inches, with 30 to 35 petals. Strong, spicy fragrance.

Form and Foliage
Medium-sized, upright plant with shiny, dark green foliage. Disease resistant.

Chicago Peace

ARS 7.7 Introduced 1962

A sport of 'Peace' that has deeper pink and yellow colors. Many prefer it over the original. Fine cut flower.

Flower and Fragrance
Large multicolored buds open into huge, deep pink flowers with yellow at the base, suffused with orange and yellow throughout. Double, 5 to 5-1/2 inches, with 50 to 60 petals. Slight fruity fragrance.

Form and Foliage
Vigorous, upright plant with shiny, deep green leaves. Prone to black spot.

Chrysler Imperial

ARS 7.8 Introduced 1953, AARS 1953

One of the finest red roses when it comes to flower form, color and fragrance. Winner of the James Alexander Gamble Rose Fragrance Award in 1965, the National Gold Medal Certificate in 1957 and many other awards. Widely used as a breeding parent for modern roses. Good cut flower and exhibition rose. Best flower form and color in warm climates.

Flower and Fragrance
Well-formed, long, pointed buds open into deep crimson-red flowers with deeper shadings. Double, 4-1/2 to 5 inches, with 40 to 50 petals. Long straight stems. Intense spicy fragrance.

Form and Foliage
Vigorous but compact plant with semiglossy green leaves. Tends to mildew and produce occasional blind shoots. Also available in a climbing form.

■ ■ ■

The American Rose Society Ratings

10	Perfect
9.9 to 9.0	Superior
8.9 to 8.0	Very Good
7.9 to 7.0	Good
6.9 to 6.0	Average
5.9 to 5.0	Poor
4.9 or below	Very Poor

Note that roses that have a blank space following the ARS rating are recent introductions and have not been in cultivation long enough to receive a rating. See page 35 for a list of the highest-rated roses.

■ ■ ■

Above: 'Brigadoon' is a tall, upright hybrid tea with rich blends of coral pink. Widely adapted with good disease resistance.

Above right: 'Dynasty' is a great hybrid tea for cutting.

Right: 'Color Magic' is a large rose with a changing personality: light pink buds open into deep pink blossoms that gradually darken to red. Excellent cut flower. Needs protection in coldest climates.

Left: 'Chicago Peace' is a sport of `Peace' (see page 75) with deeper pink and yellow flower colors. It makes a fine cut flower.

Below left: 'Chrysler Imperial' is one of the finest red roses when it comes to flower form, color and fragrance. Widely used as a breeding parent for modern roses. Best flower form and color in warm climates.

Below: 'Dainty Bess' is a pink beauty with dogwoodlike blossoms. It is one of the most popular single roses.

■ ■ ■

**Roses Susceptible to
Black Spot Disease**

Chicago Peace
Dynasty
First Prize
Garden Party
Gold Medal
Peace
Prima Donna
Simplicity

■ ■ ■

Color Magic ARS 8.2 Introduced 1978, AARS 1978

A large rose with a changing personality: light pink buds open into deep pink blossoms that gradually darken to red. Excellent cut flower. Needs protection in coldest climates.

Flower and Fragrance
Large, oval, pink buds open into huge, darker pink blossoms. Petals fade to red before falling. Double, 6 to 7 inches, with 20 to 30 petals. Strong, sweet fragrance.

Form and Foliage
Upright, well branched with full form. Dark green, semiglossy foliage. Good disease resistance.

Dainty Bess ARS 8.3 Introduced 1925

This pink beauty with dogwoodlike blossoms is one of the most popular single roses. Blooms continuously. Distinctive cut flower, although blooms are short-lived.

Flower and Fragrance
Medium pink buds, usually borne in clusters, open into clear pink blossoms with dark red stamens. Single, 3 to 4 inches, with 5 petals. Light fragrance.

Form and Foliage
Compact, upright plant with dark green, leathery leaves. Stems are very thorny. Cold hardy. Tends to get rust disease. Also available in a climbing form.

Dolly Parton ARS 7.4 Introduced 1984

A coppery, orange-red rose that performs well in hot-summer climates. Flowers are long-lasting on the bush and in the vase.

Flower and Fragrance

Nicely shaped, deep orange buds open into classic, high-centered, orange-red blosssoms. Double, 4 to 5 inches, with 35 to 40 petals. Strong, spicy fragrance.

Form and Foliage
Vigorous, densely branched, medium-sized plant with glossy green leaves. Susceptible to mildew disease.

Double Delight ARS 8.9 Introduced 1977, AARS 1977

Striking, clean white blossoms are blushed with strawberry red. This and the flower's alluring fragrance make it the most popular hybrid tea of the last 20 years. Wonderful cut flower.

Flower and Fragrance
Abundant, large white buds edged with red open into white flowers with deepening red markings. Double, 5 to 6 inches, with 40 petals. Spicy fragrance.

Form and Foliage
Bushy, medium-sized plant with good vigor. Dark green leaves. Fair winter hardiness and disease resistance. Also available in a climbing form but it is sparse-blooming.

Duet

ARS 7.6 Introduced 1961, AARS 1961

A ruffled pink blend with salmon-pink centers and reddish pink reverse. Free-flowering plant useful as hedge or container plant. Widely adapted and disease resistant. Stunning cut flower.

Flower and Fragrance
Ovoid buds open into high-pointed, light and dark pink, bicolored blossoms. Double, 4 to 5 inches, with 25 to 35 petals. Slight tea fragrance.

Form and Foliage
Vigorous, densely branched, upright plant with heavily toothed, dark green foliage.

Dynasty

ARS 7.3 Introduced 1989

A vibrant-colored, orange and yellow rose, with long-stemmed, beautifully shaped blooms. Great cut flower. Free-blooming.

Flower and Fragrance
Long, pointed buds swirl open into large, orange and yellow, bicolored blooms. Double, 4 to 5 inches, with 30 petals. Slight fragrance.

Form and Foliage
Vigorous, upright plant with semiglossy leaves. Fair disease resistance but susceptible to black spot.

Eclipse

ARS 5.6 Introduced 1935

An old-fashioned yellow rose that has withstood the test of time. Named for the solar eclipse that took place in 1932. Winner of many awards.

Flower and Fragrance
Long, slender, yellow buds open into loose, clear yellow blossoms. Double, 3-1/2 to 4 inches, with 25 to 30 petals. Slight fruity fragrance.

Form and Foliage
Upright, vigorous plant. Dark green, leathery leaves.

First Prize

ARS 8.9 Introduced 1970, AARS 1970

One of the highest-rated roses. Exquisitely formed pink flowers are tops for bouquets.

Flower and Fragrance
Large, long, pointed, pink buds open into beautiful, high-centered, rose-pink blossoms. Double, 6 inches, with 30 to 35 petals. Light fragrance.

Form and Foliage
Vigorous, spreading plant with full form. Dark green, leathery leaves are prone to mildew and black spot. Needs protection in coldest climates. Also available in a climbing form.

■ ■ ■

Roses Susceptible to Mildew

American Spirit
Apricot Nectar
Betty Prior
Caribbean
Chrysler Imperial
Dolly Parton
First Prize
Fragrant Cloud
Garden Party
Granada
Holy Toledo
Joseph's Coat
Midas Touch
Neon Lights
Oklahoma
Prima Donna
Red Cascade
Royal Highness
Sheer Bliss
Sundowner
Tropicana
Unforgettable

■ ■ ■

Above: 'Granada' is a winner of the Gamble Rose Fragrance Award, with a strong, spicy fragrance. Cut flowers are long-lasting.

Above right: 'Fragrant Memory' is grown for its large, medium pink flowers that emit a heady fragrance.

Right: 'First Prize' is one of the highest-rated roses. Large, long, pointed, pink buds open into beautiful, high-centered, rose-pink blossoms.

Fragrant Cloud   ARS 8.3 Introduced 1968

A wonderfully fragrant, coral-orange rose that is the recipient of many awards, including the Gamble Rose Fragrance Award (1969). Easy to grow and fairly disease resistant. Great cut flower. See cover photo.

Flower and Fragrance
Nicely formed, scarlet-orange buds open into classic coral-orange blossoms. Double, 4-1/2 to 5 inches, with 25 to 30 petals. Strong, spicy, sweet fragrance.

Form and Foliage
Low to medium height, full-foliaged and bushy. Shiny, deep green leaves. Will get mildew.

Fragrant Memory   ARS 7.2 Introduced 1988

A medium pink rose with a heady fragrance. Also sold as 'Jadis'.

Flower and Foliage
Large, urn-shaped, pink buds open into high-centered pink flowers with a hint of lavender. Double, 4-1/2 to 5 inches, with 25 to 30 petals. Strong, old-fashioned Damask fragrance.

Form and Foliage
Vigorous, sturdy, medium-sized, upright plant with light green, leathery leaves. Fair disease resistance.

Friendship   ARS 7.4 Introduced 1978, AARS 1979

Profusely blooming pink rose with classic hybrid tea form. Wonderfully fragrant. Reliable in all climates.

Flower and Fragrance
Large, ovoid, pink buds open into large, deep pink blossoms with a touch of pinkish red on the petal's edges. Best bloom is in fall. Double, 5-1/2 to 6 inches, with 25 to 30 petals. Strong, sweet fragrance.

Form and Foliage
Strong-growing, upright plant with large, dark green leaves. Good disease resistance.

Garden Party   ARS 8.2 Introduced 1959, AARS 1960

With 'Peace' and 'Charlotte Armstrong' as parents, this creamy white rose has an artistic form that should come as no surprise. Excellent cut flower.

Flower and Fragrance
Well-formed, urn-shaped, white buds with a hint of pink open into large, creamy white blossoms. Double, 4 to 5 inches, with 25 to 30 petals. Light tea fragrance.

Form and Foliage
Tall, full-foliaged, upright plant. Large, dark green leaves have a tendency to mildew.

■ ■ ■
**Hybrid Teas That Will
Grow in Light Shade**

Brandy
Garden Party
Swarthmore
Voodoo

■ ■ ■

Glory Days

ARS ___ Introduced 1992

Huge, nicely formed, strongly fragrant blooms in shades of rose and pink. Good cut flower.

Flower and Fragrance

Long, deep pink buds swirl open into high-centered, rose and pink blended blooms. Double, 5 to 6 inches, with 30 to 40 petals. Strong fragrance.

Form and Foliage

Tall, upright plant with medium green leaves.

Graceland

ARS 7.3 Introduced 1988

A glowing yellow rose borne profusely in long-stemmed clusters on a shapely, disease-resistant plant. Best performance in moderate climates.

Flower and Fragrance

Deep yellow buds open into high-centered, bright yellow blossoms with slightly ruffled petals. Double, 4 to 5 inches, with 30 to 35 petals. Moderate fragrance.

Form and Foliage

Upright, bushy plant with shiny, deep green foliage.

Granada

ARS 7.8 Introduced 1963, AARS 1964

A colorful, red and orange blend with wonderful fragrance. Winner of the Gamble Rose Fragrance Award in 1968. Good repeat bloom. Long-lasting cut flower.

Flower and Fragrance

Large buds open into beautiful flowers best described as a tropical blend of gold, peach, pink and red. Double, 4 to 5 inches, with 20 to 25 petals. Strong spicy fragrance.

Form and Foliage

Medium-sized upright shrub. Deep green, heavily toothed foliage. Susceptible to mildew.

Honor

ARS 7.5 Introduced 1980, AARS 1980

A beautiful, long-stemmed white rose highly prized by exhibitors. Prolific producer of long-lasting flowers, on the bush or in the vase. Good disease resistance.

Flower and Fragrance

High-pointed buds open into clear white blossoms with open centers. Double, 4 to 5 inches, with 18 to 25 petals. Light tea fragrance.

Form and Foliage

Tall-growing, upright plant. Large, deep green leaves.

Ivory Tower
ARS 7.6 Introduced 1978

Nicely formed white rose with subtle pink overtones. Good cut flower. Does best with heat.

Flower and Fragrance
Large, light pink, pointed buds open into ivory-white blossoms with a dusting of soft pink. Double, 5 to 5-1/2 inches, with 30 to 40 petals. Moderate spicy fragrance.

Form and Foliage
Tall, vigorous plant with dark green, leathery leaves.

John F. Kennedy
ARS 5.9 Introduced 1965

A white rose with an unusual touch of green in the center that fades as the blossoms mature. Performs best in hot climates.

Flower and Fragrance
Ovoid white buds tinged with green open into white blossoms with slowly fading green centers. Double, 5 to 5-1/2 inches, with 45 to 50 petals. Moderately strong fragrance.

Form and Foliage
Vigorous, upright, medium-sized bush. Medium green, leathery leaves.

Just Joey
ARS 7.7 Introduced 1972

A rich, apricot orange rose originating in Europe. It is particularly popular in the southwest U.S. where it is reliably disease resistant. Less reliable elsewhere. Wonderfully fragrant and free-blooming.

Flower and Fragrance
Shapely, brandy-colored buds open into large, apricot-orange blossoms with ruffled petals. Double, 5 inches, with 25 to 30 petals. Strong fruity fragrance.

Form and Foliage
Vigorous, medium-sized, rounded plant with glossy, deep green leaves.

King's Ransom
ARS 6.3 Introduced 1961, AARS 1962

A reliable, large, golden yellow rose. Widely adapted, but does tend to mildew in some areas. Good cut flower.

Flower and Fragrance
Long, pointed buds open slowly into loose, golden yellow blossoms. Double, 5 to 6 inches, with 40 to 45 petals. Moderately strong, sweet fragrance.

Form and Foliage
Well-branched, vigorous, upright plant clothed in deep green leaves.

■ ■ ■

**Natural Garden Tip
Plants That Attract
Beneficial Insects**

Low-growing
Aster
Catnip
Ivy
Marigold
Rosemary
Sweet clover
Thyme
White clover
Yarrow (dwarf forms)

Tall-growing
Angelica
Anise
Caraway
Dill
Fennel
Goldenrod
Mustard
Queen Anne's lace
Sunflower
Yarrow

■ ■ ■

Above: 'Graceland' is a glowing yellow rose, with flowers borne profusely in long-stemmed clusters. Moderate fragrance.

Above right: 'Ivory Tower' is a nicely formed white rose with subtle pink overtones. Moderately spicy fragrance.

Right: 'Just Joey', originating in Europe, is a rich, apricot-colored rose that performs exceptionally well in the southwest U.S.

Far right: 'Las Vegas' flowers are a colorful blend of reddish orange, cream and yellow. Plant is tall-growing and vigorous.

Left: 'Honor' is a beautiful, long-stemmed white rose highly prized by exhibitors for its prolific, long-lasting flowers.

Below left: 'Mister Lincoln' ranks with 'Chrysler Imperial', one of its parents, as among the superior fragrant red roses. Widely adapted and good repeat bloomer. AARS winner in 1965.

Below: 'Midas Touch' is a 1994 AARS selection. The dazzling yellow flowers produce a rich, musky fragrance. Combines wonderfully with blue-flowering plants.

Lady X ARS 8.3 Introduced 1966

A soft lavender rose that may be the best in its color range. Reliable bloomer. Good cut flower. Best in cool-summer climates.

Flower and Fragrance
Slender, pale lavender buds open into large, shapely, lavender blooms with a hint of pink. Double, 4-1/2 to 5 inches, with 30 to 35 petals. Mild tea fragrance.

Form and Foliage
Tall, upright, vigorous plant with few thorns. Medium green, semiglossy leaves.

Las Vegas ARS 6.7 Introduced 1981

A colorful blend of reddish orange, cream and yellow shades. Free-blooming over a long season. Handsome, disease-resistant foliage on a tall, grandiflora-like plant.

Flower and Fragrance
Bright, orange-red buds open into rich, orange-red blossoms with yellow reverse. Double, 4 inches, with 25 to 30 petals. Moderate fragrance.

Form and Foliage
Vigorous, tall-growing plant well clothed in glossy, deep green leaves.

Medallion ARS 6.7 Introduced 1973, AARS 1973

A huge, soft apricot rose that takes on a pinkish tinge in cool climates.

Flower and Fragrance
Large, nicely formed buds open into giant apricot blooms. Double, 6 to 7 inches, with 30 to 35 petals. Sweet, fruity fragrance.

Form and Foliage
Very vigorous, upright plant with deep, dark green leaves. Needs winter protection in coldest areas.

Midas Touch ARS ___ Introduced 1994, AARS 1994

The first yellow hybrid tea to be an All-America Rose Selection in 19 years. Dazzling yellow blooms with musky fragrance. Largest flowers in cooler climates. Combines wonderfully with blue-flowering plants.

Flower and Fragrance
Long, pointed buds open into bright yellow blooms. Double, 4 inches, with 20 petals. Medium musk aroma.

Form and Foliage
Healthy, upright, well-branched plant with dark green, semiglossy leaves. Good disease resistance but will get some mildew.

Mikado

ARS 7.1 Introduced 1988, AARS 1988

A velvety, red rose suffused with yellow at the base. Long-lasting cut flower. Handsome plant with glossy, deep green foliage and good disease resistance.

Flower and Fragrance

Deep red buds open into scarlet-red blooms with yellow at the base of the petals. Double, 4 to 5 inches, with 30 to 35 petals. Light spicy fragrance.

Form and Foliage

Vigorous, medium-sized, bushy plant with dark green, glossy foliage.

Miss All-American Beauty

ARS 8.2 Introduced 1967, AARS 1968

A rich, deep pink rose with alluring tea fragrance. Best performance in hot climates. Sturdy cut flower.

Flower and Foliage

Dark pink buds open into deep pink, high-centered blossoms. Double, 5 to 6 inches, with 50 to 60 petals. Medium to strong fragrance.

Form and Foliage

Tall, upright, full-foliaged plant. Large, deep green leaves.

Mister Lincoln

ARS 8.8 Introduced 1964, AARS 1965

Ranks with 'Chrysler Imperial', one of its parents, as one of the wonderfully fragrant red roses. Widely adapted and good repeat bloomer. Exceptional cut flower and exhibition rose.

Flower and Fragrance

Beautifully formed, urn-shaped buds open into huge, deep red, high-centered blooms. Double, 4-1/2 to 6 inches, with 30 to 40 petals. Rich, heady fragrance.

Form and Foliage

Upright, bushy plant with good vigor. Dark green, shiny leaves with leathery texture.

Mon Cheri

ARS 7.1 Introduced 1982, AARS 1982

A two-toned rose that opens as salmon-pink, gradually darkening to red. Good disease resistance. Long-lasting in a vase.

Flower and Fragrance

Soft orange-pink buds open slowly into blended blossoms of salmon-pink and red. Double, 4 to 4-1/2 inches, with 35 to 40 petals. Mild, spicy fragrance.

Form and Foliage

Compact upright plant with glossy green leaves.

■ ■ ■

Sampling a Rose's Fragrance

The best time to smell roses is early to midmorning—when the sun has just reached the garden. The fragrance will be most intense when the bloom is one-quarter to two-thirds open. If you prefer a particular fragrance, keep in mind that fragrant white and yellow roses usually have nasturtium, tea, violet, or lemon scents. Fragrant orange roses usually have clove, nasturtium, tea or violet scents.

■ ■ ■

Right: 'Mikado', a red rose suffused with yellow at the base, is prized as a long-lasting cut flower. It is also a handsome plant with glossy, deep green foliage and good disease resistance.

Below: 'Olympiad' is a brilliant red rose that holds well on the plant and in the vase. Excellent disease resistance and winter hardiness.

Below right: 'Mon Cheri' is a two-toned rose that opens as salmon-pink, gradually darkening to red. Good disease resistance.

Left: 'Precious Platinum' is an exceptionally free-blooming red rose that has a long life as a cut flower.

Below left: 'Peace' is the most popular hybrid tea of all time. Released at the end of World War II, this yellow rose edged with pink became a symbol of hope. Prairie rose, *Rosa setigera,* serves as a distinctive background.

Below: 'Pristine' is an accurate description of this highly rated hybrid tea. It is excellent as a cut flower, has good disease resistance but lacks cold hardiness.

Oklahoma   ARS 6.1 Introduced 1964

One of the deepest, dark red roses—it approaches blackish red. Free-blooming. Fine cut flower. Descended from 'Chrysler Imperial' and a "sister" of 'Mister Lincoln'.

Flower and Fragrance
High-pointed buds open into the deepest of red blooms. Double, 4-1/2 to 6 inches, with 40 petals. Powerful, musky aroma.

Form and Foliage
Vigorous, bushy plant with leathery, dull green foliage. Tends to mildew.

Olympiad   ARS 9.1 Introduced 1984, AARS 1984

A velvety, brilliant red rose that holds well on the plant and in the vase. Excellent disease resistance and winter hardiness.

Flower and Fragrance
Beautifully formed buds open into rich red, classic, high-centered, hybrid tea blooms. Double, 4 to 4-1/2 inches, with 25 to 30 petals. Light fragrance.

Form and Foliage
Compact, upright plant with good vigor. Semiglossy, medium green leaves on thorny stems.

Oregold   ARS 6.7 Introduced 1975, AARS 1975

A prolific producer of nicely formed, deep, yellow-gold blossoms. Beautiful cut flower.

Flower and Fragrance
Large, pointed, golden yellow buds spiral open into deep yellow blossoms. Double, 5 to 6 inches, with 35 to 40 petals. Light, fruity fragrance.

Form and Foliage
Medium-sized, full-foliaged bush with good vigor. Leaves are dark green and glossy.

Paradise   ARS 8.3 Introduced 1978, AARS 1979

A clean, crisp, lavender rose edged with ruby-red. The first and only lavender hybrid tea to win AARS. Long-lasting cut flower. Excellent disease resistance.

Flower and Fragrance
Beautifully shaped, reddish lavender buds open into perfectly formed, high-centered, lavender flowers edged with deep red. Double, 5 inches, with 25 to 30 petals. Moderate, fruity fragrance.

Form and Foliage
Handsome, full-foliaged, medium-sized plant with glossy, deep green leaves.

Party Time
ARS 7.0 Introduced 1987

An ever-changing bicolor of yellow edged with deep rose-red. Prolific bloom. Long-lasting on the plant and as a cut flower. Excellent disease resistance.

Flower and Fragrance
Large, round buds open into yellow flowers edged with pinkish red. Double, 4 inches, with 25 to 30 petals. Light fragrance.

Form and Foliage
Vigorous upright plant. Semiglossy, medium green leaves.

Pascali
ARS 8.1 Introduced 1968, AARS 1969

Perfectly formed crystal white flowers, excellent disease resistance and generous production throughout summer make this one of the most popular and highly regarded white roses. Flowers are smaller in warm-summer regions.

Flower and Fragrance
Classically shaped buds open into creamy white blossoms. Double, 3 to 4 inches, with 30 petals. Slight tea fragrance.

Form and Foliage
Medium-sized, upright, vigorous grower. Dark green, glossy leaves.

Peace
ARS 8.6 Introduced 1945, AARS 1946

The most popular hybrid tea of all time. Released at the end of World War II, this yellow rose edged with pink became a symbol of hope. Blossoms are perfectly formed and long-lasting when cut. Winner of numerous awards such as ARS National Gold Medal and the Portland Gold Medal.

Flower and Fragrance
Large, oval, yellow buds open into huge yellow blossoms with petals tipped in pink. Double, 5 to 6 inches, with 40 to 45 petals. Light fragrance.

Form and Foliage
Tall, vigorous plant with glossy, deep green leaves. Susceptible to black spot. Also available in a climbing form.

Perfect Moment
ARS 7.5 Introduced 1991, AARS 1991

Striking yellow blooms with broad red edgings on the outside of the petals. Free-blooming with strong stems. Good cut flower.

Flower and Fragrance
Medium, pointed buds open into yellow blooms, edged red. Double, 4 to 4-1/2 inches, with 35 petals. Slight fruity fragrance.

Form and Foliage
Upright medium-sized plant with dark green leaves. Good to excellent disease resistance.

■ ■ ■

Disease-Resistant Hybrid Teas

Brigadoon
Broadway
Color Magic
Friendship
Graceland
Just Joey
Midas Touch
Mikado
Mon Cheri
Olympiad
Paradise
Party Time
Perfect Moment
Rio Samba
Secret
Sheer Elegance
Voodoo

■ ■ ■

Perfume Delight
ARS 7.6 Introduced 1974, AARS 1974

Intensely fragrant pink rose with 'Chrysler Imperial' heritage. Free-blooming, disease resistant and beautiful as a cut flower.

Flower and Fragrance
Bright pink, high-pointed buds open into cup-shaped, velvety pink blossoms. Double, 4-1/2 to 5 inches. About 30 petals. Strong, old-fashioned fragrance.

Form and Foliage
Medium-sized, vigorous plant with leathery, dull green leaves

Precious Platinum
ARS 7.5 Introduced 1974

An exceptionally free-blooming red rose that has a long life as a cut flower. Performs best in northwest U.S.

Flower and Fragrance
High-centered buds open into cardinal red blossoms. Double, 3-1/2 inches, with 35 to 40 petals. Slight fragrance.

Form and Foliage
Vigorous upright plant with dark green, glossy foliage. Disease resistant.

Princesse de Monaco
ARS 7.4 Introduced 1981

A white rose with pink edges that is said to have been a favorite of Princess Grace because its colors are the same as those on the flag of Monaco. Good cut flower.

Flower and Fragrance
White buds tipped with pink open into high-centered white flowers with pink edgings. Double, 4-1/2 inches, with 30 to 35 petals. Light fragrance.

Form and Foliage
Medium-sized, upright plant with full foliage. Deep green, semiglossy leaves.

Pristine
ARS 9.2 Introduced 1978

"Pristine" aptly describes this porcelain white rose with soft pink edges. Has good disease resistance but lacks cold hardiness.

Flower and Fragrance
Shapely, bright white buds with a hint of pink open into clear white blossoms with a dusting of pink on the outer petals. Double, 5 to 6 inches, with 25 to 30 petals. Light fragrance.

Form and Foliage
Coarse, medium to tall plant, with good vigor. Deep green leaves have a reddish tinge.

Opposite, top left: 'Red Devil' is a good choice for cool climates. Large, round buds open into beautiful, bright red flowers with silvery red undersides.

Top right: 'Rio Samba' is a 1993 AARS award winner. The shocking yellow blooms blushed with bright orange create a festive mood. Best color occurs in cool climates.

Bottom left: 'Princesse de Monaco' is an attractive white rose with bright pink edges. A good cut flower with light fragrance.

Bottom right: 'Secret' is a 1994 AARS winner, with excellent disease resistance, especially against mildew.

The climate you live in has a significant influence on how tall or wide your roses will grow. For example, the long growing season in Southern California and the Deep South allows roses to grow almost year-around. Left unpruned during the summer, a hybrid tea may reach 6 to 8 feet high. By comparison, the growing season in cold-winter climates such as the upper Midwest may be 3 to 4 months long. The same variety of hybrid tea may only reach 3 to 4 feet high.

■ ■ ■

Red Devil   ARS 7.2 Introduced 1970

A good choice for cooler climates. Flowers open poorly in hot weather. Good cut flower.

Flower and Fragrance
Large round buds open into beautiful, bright red flowers with silvery red undersides. Double, 3-1/2 inches, with up to 70 petals. Slight fragrance.

Form and Foliage
Extremely vigorous and upright. Glossy green foliage.

Rio Samba   ARS ___ Introduced 1993, AARS 1993

Shocking yellow blooms blushed with bright orange. Flowers are often borne in clusters. Best color occurs in cool climates.

Flower and Fragrance
Pointed, oval buds open into yellow blooms blushing to orange. Double, 5 inches, with 25 to 30 petals. Light fragrance.

Form and Foliage
Medium to tall, upright plant with medium green leaves. Good disease resistance.

Royal Amethyst   ARS 7.6 Introduced 1989

Large lavender blooms with fruity fragrance.

Flower and Fragrance
Pointed buds open into large lavender blooms. Double, 4 to 5 inches, with 30 to 35 petals. Heavy, fruity fragrance.

Form and Foliage
Medium-sized, upright plant with glossy, medium green leaves.

Royal Highness   ARS 8.2 Introduced 1962, AARS 1963

A classically formed, light pink rose that has won many awards for its perfectly shaped blossoms. Free-blooming. Excellent cut flower. Top exhibition rose. Needs winter protection in coldest climates.

Flower and Fragrance
Long, pointed, soft pink buds open into high-centered, light pink blossoms. Double, 5 to 5-1/2 inches, with 40 to 50 petals. Strong fragrance.

Form and Foliage
Vigorous, upright, full-foliaged plant. Dark green, semiglossy leaves. Susceptible to rust and mildew.

Seashell
ARS 6.8 Introduced 1976, AARS 1976

A peach-pink, apricot-orange and cream blend. Good disease resistance; winter hardy.

Flower and Fragrance
Large, soft orange buds open into high-centered, blended flowers with shades of pink, orange and cream. Double, 4 to 5 inches, with 45 to 50 petals.

Form and Foliage
Upright and vigorous with dark green, glossy leaves.

Secret
ARS __ Introduced 1994, AARS 1994

Beautiful cream blooms edged with soft pink. Alluring, sweet, spicy fragrance. Long-stemmed cut flower. Good disease resistance, especially against mildew.

Flower and Fragrance
High-centered, pointed buds open into creamy white blooms edged with coral pink. Double, 4-1/2 inches, with 30 to 35 petals. Strong, spicy, fruity fragrance.

Form and Foliage
Medium to large, bushy plant with semiglossy, medium green leaves. Good disease resistance.

Sheer Bliss
ARS 7.8 Introduced 1987, AARS 1987

A delicate cream-white rose with a soft pink center and spicy fragrance. Reliable bloomer that is easy to grow.

Flower and Fragrance
Long, pointed, cream-white buds swirl open into white flowers with light pink centers. Double, 4 to 5 inches, with 30 to 35 petals. Moderately strong, spicy fragrance.

Form and Foliage
Medium-tall, slightly spreading plant with glossy, deep green leaves. Susceptible to rust and mildew.

Sheer Elegance
ARS 7.7 Introduced 1991, AARS 1991

Delicate soft pink blooms edged with darker pink make wonderful cut flowers. Excellent disease resistance. Colors best in areas with warm nights.

Flower and Fragrance
Medium, pointed buds open into cream-pink, cupped blooms edged with darker pink. Double, 4 to 5 inches, with 35 to 45 petals. Moderate to strong musk aroma.

Form and Foliage
Medium-sized, upright plant with dark green leaves. Excellent disease resistance.

Right: 'Touch of Class' is a highly rated rose, grown for its coral-pink blooms. Exceptionally long lasting as a cut flower.

Below: 'Tiffany' is a popular and easy-to-grow hybrid tea, with good disease resistance. One of the most fragrant of all roses.

Below right: 'Voodoo' is another easy-to-grow rose that is disease resistant. Fragrance is strong and fruity.

Summer Dream

ARS 7.7 Introduced 1987

Huge, beautifully colored rose. Primarily apricot pink but in warm climates orange-tipped petals become yellow at the base. Plant is free-blooming and disease resistant.

Flower and Fragrance
Large, pink buds open into pink blossoms marked with yellow and orange. Double, 6 to 7 inches, with 25 to 30 petals. Light fragrance.

Form and Foliage
Tall, vigorous plant with handsome, deep green, glossy foliage.

Summer Sunshine

ARS 6.6 Introduced 1962

A dependable, deep yellow hybrid tea. Fair disease resistance but needs winter protection in coldest climates.

Flower and Fragrance
Nicely shaped buds open into deep yellow blossoms. Double, 5 inches, with 25 to 30 petals. Mild fragrance.

Form and Foliage
Medium-sized, somewhat spreading plant with gray-green, leathery leaves.

Sutter's Gold

ARS 5.7 Introduced 1950, AARS 1950

A favorite yellow rose with red shadings on the outer petals. Highly regarded for bud form and fragrance, as witnessed by its many awards, including the Gamble Rose Fragrance Award in 1966. Disease resistant.

Flower and Fragrance
Long, tapered, golden buds with just a hint of red open into high-centered, somewhat loose, gold blossoms with a red blush. Double, 4 to 5 inches, with 30 to 35 petals. Very strong, fruity fragrance.

Form and Foliage
Upright, vigorous and full-foliaged. Dark green, leathery leaves. Also available in a climbing form.

Swarthmore

ARS 8.1 Introduced 1963

A prolific-blooming rose-red hybrid tea that has a long life on the plant or in the vase. Does best in regions with warm summer nights.

Flower and Fragrance
Long, pointed buds open into rose-red blossoms edged with darker red. Double, 4 inches, with 45 to 55 petals. Slight spicy fragrance.

Form and Foliage
Strong-growing, sturdy plant of medium height. Dark green, leathery leaves.

■ ■ ■

Long-Lasting Cut Roses

As reported by the American Rose Society, these roses are among the best varieties for long-lasting cut flowers. To prolong the length of time that cut roses look attractive, use a floral preservative or add a clear, citrus-based soda, one part to three parts water.

Red roses
Mister Lincoln
Olé
Olympiad
Viva

Pink roses
America
Bewitched
Cherish
Color Magic
Sonia
Touch of Class
Voodoo

Purple roses
Deep Purple
Intrigue
Paradise

White roses
Honor
Iceberg
Pascali

■ ■ ■

Sweet Surrender
ARS 6.6 Introduced 1983, AARS 1983

A silvery pink rose that resembles an old-fashioned cabbage-type rose.

Flower and Fragrance
Large, pointed buds open into flat-topped, medium pink blossoms with silvery shadings. Double, 3-1/2 to 4-1/2 inches, with 40 to 45 petals. Strong tea fragrance.

Form and Foliage
Medium-sized, upright bush with large, dark green leaves. May need winter protection in coldest areas.

Tiffany
ARS 8.3 Introduced 1954, AARS 1955

A much-loved pink rose that is one of the most popular and easy-to-grow hybrid teas. Winner of many awards, including the Gamble Rose Fragrance Award in 1962. Great cut flower.

Flower and Fragrance
High-pointed, deep pink buds open into satiny pink blossoms with yellow shadings at the base of the petals. Double, 4 to 5 inches, with 25 to 30 petals. Intense, fruity fragrance.

Form and Foliage
Medium-tall, upright bush with good vigor. Dark green, glossy leaves. Good disease resistance.

Touch of Class
ARS 9.5 Introduced 1986, AARS 1987

A beautiful, coral-pink rose with orange and cream shadings. Exceptional long-stemmed cut flower with superb form.

Flower and Fragrance
Large pink buds spiral open into high-centered, coral-pink blossoms with orange and cream markings. Double, 3-1/2 to 4-1/2 inches, with about 30 petals. Slight tea fragrance.

Form and Foliage
Vigorous, medium to tall, bushy plant with deep green leaves.

Tropicana
ARS 7.9 Introduced 1962, AARS 1963

A popular variety, admired for its fluorescent, coral-orange color. Easy to grow and a prolific bloomer. Excellent as a cut flower. Winner of many awards.

Flower and Fragrance
Beautifully formed, pointed, orange-red buds open into bright, coral-orange, cup-shaped blossoms. Double, 4-1/2 to 5 inches, with 30 to 35 petals. Strong fruity fragrance.

Form and Foliage
Vigorous, tall and upright. Dark green, leathery, glossy leaves. Susceptible to mildew.

Unforgettable

ARS ___ Introduced 1991

Nicely formed, large pink blooms are borne in abundance. Lovely cut flower.

Flower and Fragrance
Long, pointed buds open into pink blooms with lightly ruffled petals. Double, 5-1/2 inches, with 35 to 40 petals. Light to moderate fragrance.

Form and Foliage
Upright, spreading plant with semiglossy, deep green leaves. Tends to mildew.

Voodoo

ARS 7.0 Introduced 1986, AARS 1987

A pretty blended rose of peachy yellow with a scarlet blush. Easy to grow; has fair disease resistance.

Flower and Fragrance
Large, orange-yellow buds open into soft, orange-yellow blossoms with a hint of scarlet. Double, 4 to 5 inches, with 30 to 35 petals. Strong fruity fragrance.

Form and Foliage
Tall, vigorous plant with handsome, deep green, glossy leaves.

White Delight

ARS 7.6 Introduced 1990

A quick-reblooming, vigorous rose with white blooms shaded with soft pink. Long-stemmed cut flower.

Flower and Fragrance
Ovoid, pointed buds open to become large, high-centered, white blooms blushed with pink. Double, 4-1/2 inches, with 35 to 40 petals. Slight fragrance.

Form and Foliage
Vigorous, upright plant with glossy, dark green leaves.

White Masterpiece

ARS 7.5 Introduced 1969

Classic white exhibition rose with good disease resistance. Often described as a "shy bloomer." Needs winter protection in coldest climates.

Flower and Fragrance
Oval buds open evenly into high-centered, pure white blossoms. Double, 5 to 6 inches, with 50 to 60 petals. Light fragrance.

Form and Foliage
Small, spreading plant with medium green, semiglossy leaves.

■ ■ ■

Natural Garden Tip

Spraying with broad-spectrum insecticides—those that are effective on all insects—reduces many natural insect predators and parasites, and can eventually result in a build-up of insect pests. Population surges of two rose pests, thrips and spider mites, are closely associated with recent insecticides applications. The reason? Not only are natural enemies killed, but newer generations of the pests have a greater resistance to the insecticide, and future applications will be less effective.

■ ■ ■

Floribundas

Versatility is the word that comes to mind when describing floribunda roses. Originally hybrids of polyanthas (compact forms of the hedgerow rose), Rosa multiflora, and hybrid teas, floribundas combine the best characteristics of each. Today, rose breeders have continued to back-cross floribundas with hybrid teas and also with other floribundas to develop some wonderfully useful flowering shrubs. Generally free-blooming, cold hardy and disease resistant, floribundas are among the best choices for landscape roses. The flowers are not quite as large as those of hybrid teas and are often borne in clusters, but they come in every rose color, and in abundance. Plants produce so many blooms they are nicknamed "flower machines."

Plants are attractive with compact growth habits, and, more often than not, shiny, deep green leaves. They range from tall and upright, reaching 5 feet high, to low, spreading varieties that are easily maintained at 2 feet high. Floribundas are most useful as hedges or borders. They are also excellent used in massed plantings and in containers or mixed with flowering perennials. Lower, spreading types can be used as ground covers or tall edgings.

Also described here are the best polyantha roses. They too are free-blooming and well suited as edgings, for low hedges, containers and combined with other flowering plants.

Opposite: A border planting of 'Eye Paint' in combination with bright green ferns makes a dramatic scene. Floribundas are among the best roses for landscape use.

Above: 'Sun Flare' is effective when used as a flowering hedge.

Left: 'Sexy Rexy' is a popular floribunda, valued for its prolific flowering and resistance to disease.

Amber Queen   ARS 6.7 Introduced 1988, AARS 1988

Soft, apricot-gold blossoms with a sweet and spicy fragrance highlight this fine floribunda. A compact and handsome landscape plant. Best performance in the West.

Flower and Fragrance

Light apricot flowers are borne in clusters that swirl open into high-centered, apricot-gold blossoms. Double, 2-1/2 to 3 inches, with 25 to 30 petals. Strong fragrance.

Form and Foliage

Low-growing, bushy plants with shiny, dark green foliage. Good disease resistance.

Angel Face   ARS 8.1 Introduced 1968, AARS 1969

Large, ruffled, lavender blossoms have a strong citrus fragrance, which earned 'Angel Face' the distinction of being the only floribunda in the lavender color range to win AARS. Good repeat bloomer. Flower color is best with some afternoon shade in hot climates.

Flower and Fragrance

High-centered buds open into cup-shaped, lavender-red blossoms with ruffled petals and bright yellow stamens. Double, 3-1/2 to 4 inches, with 25 to 30 petals. Borne mostly in clusters. Intense citrus fragrance.

Form and Foliage

Low-growing, rounded shrub with dense, dark green, semiglossy leaves. Hardy to cold.

Apricot Nectar   ARS 8.2 Introduced 1965, AARS 1966

A large-flowering, upright, soft apricot-colored floribunda. Prolific bloomer in all climates. Good cut flower.

Flower and Fragrance

Apricot-orange buds borne in clusters open into a lighter, soft apricot flower. Double, 4-1/2 to 5 inches, with 35 to 40 petals. Strong fruity fragrance.

Form and Foliage

Vigorous, upright plant with semiglossy, dark green leaves. Winter hardy and disease resistant.

Betty Prior   ARS 8.2 Introduced 1935

When you first see 'Betty Prior' in bloom, you might think it is a small, pink-flowering dogwood. Large, single, pink blooms completely cover the plant. It is a stunning sight, which is why this has been a favorite rose for well over 50 years.

Flower and Fragrance

Dark, carmine-pink buds open into bright pink blossoms with lighter pink centers and yellow stamens. Single, 2 to 3 inches, with 5 to 7 petals. Borne in clusters. Moderate tea fragrance.

Form and Foliage

Medium-sized, rounded shrub with semiglossy green leaves. Excellent disease resistance and hardiness.

Brass Band

ARS ___ Introduced 1995, AARS 1995

A beautiful floribunda with flowers in fruity shades of orange with a yellow reverse. Bright green foliage and good disease resistance. Best color in cool climates.

Flower and Fragrance
Large flowers in blended shades of orange with yellow reverse. Double, 3-1/2 to 4 inches, with 30 to 35 petals. Flowers are borne in clusters. Moderate fruity fragrance.

Form and Foliage
Medium-sized, rounded shrub with bright green leaves.

Bridal Pink

ARS 8.4 Introduced 1967

This is a free-blooming pink rose and a favorite of florists for bridal bouquets. Good cut flower and fine landscape choice.

Flower and Fragrance
Oval, pointed buds open into high-centered pink blooms. Double, 3 to 4 inches, with 30 to 35 petals. Borne in clusters. Moderately spicy fragrance.

Form and Foliage
Medium-sized plant with bushy, rounded habit. Dark green leaves.

Cathedral

ARS 7.9 Introduced 1975, AARS 1976

A gleaming, apricot-orange and salmon-pink blended rose with wavy petals. Excellent compact form. Good cut flower. Best performance in the West.

Flower and Fragrance
Apricot-orange buds open into deeper, pinkish orange blossoms that slowly deepen to scarlet. Double, 3 to 3-1/2 inches, with 18 to 24 petals. Borne in clusters. Sweet, light fragrance.

Form and Foliage
Medium-sized, compact plant with glossy, dark green leaves. Hardy and disease resistant.

Cécile Brunner

ARS 8.0 Introduced 1881

A dainty pink polyantha rose known as the *sweetheart rose* because of its traditional use as a boutonniere. Blooms continuously. Pretty cut flower.

Flower and Fragrance
Small pink buds with classic, pointed form swirl open into small but beautiful pink blossoms that have a touch of yellow at the center. Double, 1-1/2 inches, with about 30 petals. Borne in airy clusters. Moderate fragrance.

Form and Foliage
Medium-sized, bushy, somewhat spreading plant with dark green, glossy foliage. Disease resistant but needs winter protection in cold-winter regions. Climbing form blooms best in spring.

■ ■ ■

Natural Garden Tip

Downy mildew is a relatively new pest of roses. It is often confused with other diseases and is difficult to control. If you think your roses are infected, contact your local rose society, they can help you with identification and the latest control techniques.

■ ■ ■

Above: 'Amber Queen' produces soft, apricot gold flowers in clusters. The handsome, compact plant is disease resistant.

Above right: 'Angel Face' is grown for its large, ruffled lavender flowers. It is a repeat bloomer that resists disease.

Right: 'Class Act' is an easy-to-grow and profuse-flowering landscape plant. Highly disease resistant. In the background is the grandiflora 'Prima Donna'.

Left: 'Charisma' produces flowers that have an interesting blend of yellow, orange and red. Its compact growth habit, long season of bloom and disease resistance make it a highly useful landscape plant.

Below: 'China Doll', here trained as a weeping tree form, is an old-time polyantha. Small pink flowers are borne in profusion. A hardy and disease-resistant rose.

Charisma   ARS 6.9 Introduced 1977, AARS 1978

An intensely colored rose of yellow, orange and red blends. Deep green foliage, compact habit and long season of bloom make it an excellent landscape rose. Good cut flower. Best performance in the West.

Flower and Fragrance
Egg-shaped buds swirl open into nicely formed, yellow blossoms edged with orange-red, which deepens as the flower ages. Double, 2-1/2 to 3 inches, with at least 40 petals. Borne singly and in clusters. Light, fruity fragrance.

Form and Foliage
Medium-sized, compact plant with deep green, very glossy leaves. Tough and disease resistant.

Cherish   ARS 8.3 Introduced 1980, AARS 1980

A large-flowering, shell-pink floribunda. Consistent bloomer in all climates. Good cut flower. Nicely shaped landscape plant.

Flower and Fragrance
Clear pink buds open slowly into large, soft pink blooms with hybrid tea form. Double, 3 to 4 inches, with 25 to 30 petals. Borne in clusters. Mild spicy fragrance.

Form and Foliage
Vigorous, low to medium, bushy plant with a neat, round shape. Glossy, deep green leaves.

China Doll   ARS 8.3 Introduced 1946

An old-time polyantha with large clusters of small, fluffy pink blooms. A small, compact plant that makes an excellent edging, low border or container plant. Free-blooming.

Flower and Fragrance
Small pink buds open into clear pink, cup-shaped blooms with ruffled petals. Double, 1 to 2 inches, with 20 to 25 petals. Borne in large clusters. Light fragrance.

Form and Foliage
Low-growing, mound-shaped plant that usually reaches about 1-1/2 feet high. Bright green, leathery leaves. Disease resistant and hardy. Also available as a climbing form.

Class Act   ARS 7.5 Introduced 1989, AARS 1989

Aptly named, this is an outstanding, easy-to-grow white rose that seems to never cease flowering. An exceptional landscape plant. Highly disease resistant. Best performance in the West.

Flower and Fragrance
Perfectly shaped, cream-white buds open into high-centered, pristine white blossoms. Double, 4 inches, with 20 to 25 petals. Borne in clusters. Light, fruity fragrance.

Form and Foliage
Vigorous, medium-sized, rounded shrub with dark green leaves.

Europeana
ARS 9.0 Introduced 1968, AARS 1968

This is the standard of excellence for red floribundas. An exceptional, easy-to-grow landscape plant with compact spreading habit and nonstop blooms.

Flower and Fragrance
Pointed, deep red buds open into deep crimson blossoms. Double, 3 to 3-1/2 inches, with 25 to 30 petals. Borne in large clusters. Light fragrance.

Form and Foliage
Low-growing, spreading plant with deep green, glossy foliage. Excellent disease resistance and winter hardiness.

Evening Star
ARS 8.2 Introduced 1974

Called a *flora tea rose* by the nursery that introduced it, 'Evening Star' bears long-stemmed, hybrid tea-like, white blossoms on a compact plant that is more like a floribunda. A carefree landscape plant. Fine cut flower.

Flower and Fragrance
Pure white buds open into large, bright white blossoms. Double, 4 to 5 inches, with 35 petals. Borne singly and in small clusters. Light fragrance.

Form and Foliage
Medium to tall, compact, bushy, with deep green leaves. Needs winter protection in cold climates.

Eye Paint
ARS 8.1 Introduced 1975

'Eye Paint' is an eye-catching, red and white, single floribunda with bright yellow stamens. It produces abundant flowers. Makes a nice hedge or climber.

Flower and Fragrance
Ovoid buds open into bright red blossoms with white centers and golden yellow stamens. Single, 2-1/2 inches, with 5 to 7 petals. Borne in clusters. Slight fragrance.

Form and Foliage
Tall, upright, bushy plant is densely covered in small, dark green leaves. Has the appearance of an old-time shrub rose.

First Edition
ARS 8.6 Introduced 1976, AARS 1977

A beauty in flower and foliage. Blossoms are dark coral-orange with shadings of pink, red and yellow. The plant is compact and attractive, ideal for a hedge or in containers. Best color in cooler climates. Great cut flower.

Flower and Fragrance
Pointed, urn-shaped buds open into coral-orange blossoms often blended with red, pink or yellow. Double, 2-1/2 to 3 inches, with 25 to 30 petals. Borne singly or in clusters. Mild tea fragrance.

Form and Foliage
Medium-sized, dense, rounded shrub with light green, glossy leaves. Provide winter protection in coldest climates.

Right: 'Eye Paint' is an eye-catcher, with its single red and white blooms set off by bright yellow stamens. Flowers profusely. Also see photo on page 84.

Below: 'French Lace' begins flowering with pointed, cream-white buds that open into white blossoms tinged with pale yellow. A disease-resistant rose.

Below right: 'Europeana' is the standard of excellence for red floribundas. It's a highly rated, easy-to-grow plant, possessing excellent disease resistance and cold hardiness.

Above left: 'Gene Boerner' is a pink-flowering floribunda named for one of the world's finest rose breeders. A versatile plant, it can be used as a hedge or for cutting, and is hardy and disease resistant.

Above: 'First Edition' is a dense, compact, medium-sized plant, with attractive flowers and foliage. Provide with winter protection in coldest regions.

Left: 'Iceberg' is considered a workhorse rose, blooming almost nonstop through the season. Plant is hardy and disease resistant. See additional photos on pages 25 and 29.

■ ■ ■

**Floribundas That Will
Grow in Light Shade**

Angel Face
French Lace
Regensberg

■ ■ ■

First Kiss

ARS 7.6 Introduced 1991

A light pink floribunda derived from a cross of 'Sun Flare' and 'Simplicity'. The combination of compact growth and everblooming habit make it a superior landscape rose.

Flower and Fragrance

Pointed, ovoid buds open into soft pink blooms with yellow base. Double, 3-1/2 to 4 inches, with 20 to 25 petals. Borne in clusters. Slight fragrance.

Form and Foliage

Upright, rounded form with deep green leaves.

French Lace

ARS 8.2 Introduced 1982, AARS 1982

A hybrid tea-like floribunda, bearing cream-white flowers with a hint of pale yellow. Easy to grow; produces generous blooms. Accepts some shade.

Flower and Fragrance

Pointed, cream-white buds open into high-centered, white blossoms with a hint of apricot-yellow. Double, 3-1/2 to 4 inches, with 30 to 35 petals. Borne singly and in clusters. Mild, fruity fragrance.

Form and Foliage

Medium to tall, bushy, with dark green foliage. Good disease resistance.

Frensham

ARS 6.6 Introduced 1946

One of the oldest floribundas, 'Frensham' gets its classic hybrid tea-like, red flowers from one of its parents, 'Crimson Glory'. Good repeat bloomer.

Flower and Fragrance

Pointed, dark red buds open into deep crimson, cup-shaped flowers. Semidouble, 3 inches, with 15 petals. Borne in large clusters. Slight fragrance.

Form and Foliage

Vigorous, medium-sized, slightly spreading plant with dark green leaves. Good disease resistance and winter hardiness.

Gene Boerner

ARS 8.5 Introduced 1969, AARS 1969

This long-lasting, pure pink floribunda carries the name of one of the world's finest rose breeders. It is a tall, upright plant that seems to be constantly in bloom. Excellent hedge rose and good cut flower.

Flower and Fragrance

Pink, hybrid tea-like buds open into high-centered, bright pink blossoms. Double, 3 to 3-1/2 inches, with 35 to 40 petals. Borne singly and in clusters. Light spicy fragrance.

Form and Foliage

Very vigorous, upright plant is well covered with glossy green leaves. Excellent hardiness and disease resistance.

Gingersnap

ARS 7.1 Introduced 1978

A bright orange rose with hints of yellow in its ruffly petals. 'Gingersnap' is an eye-catching landscape rose, ideal as hedge or border. Tender to cold, so best suited to mild-winter regions. See phogo page 23.

Flower and Fragrance
Long, pointed, orange buds open into bright orange blooms with a touch of yellow at the base of the ruffled petals. Double, 4 to 4-1/2 inches, with 30 to 35 petals. Borne singly or in clusters. Mild fragrance.

Form and Foliage
Medium-sized, bushy plant with deep green, glossy leaves.

Iceberg

ARS 8.7 Introduced 1958

The standard of excellence for white floribundas. Perfect in almost every way, with abundant bloom all season long on a bushy, disease-resistant plant. Truly a superior landscape rose.

Flower and Fragrance
Slender, long, pointed buds open into pure white blossoms. Double, 3 inches, with 20 to 25 petals. Borne in clusters. Mild, honeylike fragrance.

Form and Foliage
Vigorous, medium to tall, upright bush with dense, shiny, deep green leaves. Excellent disease resistance and hardiness.

Impatient

ARS 7.8 Introduced 1984, AARS 1984

A glowing, orange-red rose. Free-blooming habit and clean, glossy foliage make it a handsome landscape plant.

Flower and Fragrance
Deep, orange-red buds unfurl into well-formed, orange-red blossoms. Double, 3 inches, with 20 to 30 petals. Borne singly or in small clusters. Light, spicy fragrance.

Form and Foliage
Medium to tall, upright bush with deep green, semiglossy foliage. Good disease resistance and winter hardiness.

Intrigue

ARS 6.8 Introduced 1984, AARS 1984

A unique, plum-purple rose with heady fragrance. Very free-blooming. Good cut flower. An unusual accent plant combined with white or pink roses.

Flower and Fragrance
Pointed buds open into high-centered, reddish purple blossoms. Double, 3 inches, with 25 to 30 petals. Borne singly and in clusters. Strong citrus fragrance.

Form and Foliage
Medium-sized, upright plant with shiny, dark green leaves.

■ ■ ■
Floribundas with Fragrance

Amber Queen
Angel Face
Apricot Nectar
Iceberg
Intrigue
Judy Garland
Margaret Merrill
Neon Lights
Regensberg
Rose Parade
Saratoga
Sunsprite

■ ■ ■

Ivory Fashion
ARS 8.6 Introduced 1959, AARS 1959

Ivory-white blossoms with fruity fragrance have made this a favorite floribunda for years. A fine landscape plant.

Flower and Fragrance
Crystal white buds open into clear white blossoms with yellow stamens. Semidouble, 3-1/2 to 4 inches, with 15 to 20 petals. Borne in clusters. Moderate fruity fragrance.

Form and Foliage
Medium-sized, upright, densely branched plant with medium green, leathery leaves. Disease resistant and winter hardy.

Judy Garland
ARS 7.4 Introduced 1978

A multicolored floribunda with flowers in shades of yellow, orange and red. Very fragrant and free-blooming.

Flower and Fragrance
Urn-shaped buds open into yellow blooms edged with orange and red. Double, 2-1/2 to 3-1/2 inches, with 30 to 35 petals. Born in clusters. Strong fruity fragrance.

Form and Foliage
Medium to large, compact plant with semiglossy dark green leaves.

Little Darling
ARS 8.6 Introduced 1956

A delightful yellow and salmon-pink blend. Prolific bloomer. Tall, spreading growth habit—good as a hedge. Nice cut flower.

Flower and Fragrance
Delicate oval buds open into cup-shaped, yellow and salmon-pink blended blossoms. Double, 2-1/2 inches, with 24 to 30 petals. Borne in clusters. Spicy fragrance.

Form and Foliage
Vigorous, slightly spreading plant with deep green, glossy leaves. Disease-resistant and winter hardy.

Margaret Merrill
ARS 8.0 Introduced 1978

A multiple award winner prized for its wonderful fragrance and lovely white flowers that have a trace of a pink blush. A great landscape rose, with a low, compact habit and disease-resistant foliage. A fine choice for a free-blooming low hedge or for use in combination plantings. Sometimes sold as a shrub rose.

Flower and Fragrance
High-centered buds open into ruffled white blossoms with shades of light pink. Double, 4 inches, with 25 to 30 petals. Borne in clusters. Intense lemon and spice fragrance.

Form and Foliage
Low-growing, compact plant with deep green foliage.

Opposite, far left: 'Marina', an AARS selection in 1981, is a glowing orange rose tinged with gold and salmon. The flower form is prized by florists.

Left: 'Ivory Fashion' is a time-honored floribunda, awarded AARS in 1959. Ivory-white flowers have a fruity fragrance. The medium-sized, upright plant has a variety of uses in the landscape.

Bottom: A climbing form of the polyantha 'Margo Koster' is in the process of covering a chain-link fence. Introduced in 1931, this rose remains a favorite of rose growers as well as florists.

Margo Koster

ARS 8.3 Introduced 1931

A longtime favorite for containers, this coral-orange polyantha is often sold by florists. Good repeat bloom. Low growing and compact, it also makes a nice edging or low border.

Flower and Fragrance
Small, salmon-pink buds open into cup-shaped, coral blooms. Double, 1 to 1-1/2 inches, with 20 to 25 petals. Borne in clusters. Slight fragrance.

Form and Foliage
Small, compact plant usually grows to about 1 foot high. Glossy, deep green leaves. Also available as a climbing form.

Marina

ARS 7.7 Introduced 1980, AARS 1981

A glowing, orange rose with flushes of gold and salmon. The beautifully formed flower is long-lasting in the vase and prized by florists.

Flower and Fragrance
Nicely shaped buds open into large, hybrid tea-like, orange blossoms with golden yellow bases and hints of salmon. Double, 2-1/2 to 3 inches, with 35 to 40 petals. Borne singly and in clusters. Moderate fruity fragrance.

Form and Foliage
Medium to tall, upright plant with dark green, glossy leaves.

Neon Lights

ARS ___ Introduced 1992

A free-blooming, bright magenta-pink rose with ruffled petals, a tight, compact habit, and fair disease resistance. Great landscape shrub with strong fragrance.

Flower and Fragrance
Long, slender pink buds open into full magenta pink blossoms. Double, 4 to 4-1/2 inches, with 25 to 30 petals. Flowers are borne in clusters. Strong fragrance.

Form and Foliage
Medium-sized, compact plant with semiglossy foliage. Susceptible to mildew.

New Year

ARS 6.2 Introduced 1983, AARS 1987

A festive orange and yellow blended rose imported from New Zealand. Full-foliaged plant with good disease resistance. Good cut flower.

Flower and Fragrance
Nicely formed buds open into orange and yellow blended blooms. Double, 3-1/2 to 4-1/2 inches, with 25 petals. Slight fruity fragrance.

Form and Foliage
Medium-sized, upright, bushy plant with glossy, deep green leaves.

Origami

ARS ___ Introduced 1991

A perfectly formed floribunda that produces pink blushed with coral flowers that have a delightful fragrance. Performs well in all conditions, although warm weather brings out the best color. Good cut flower.

Flower and Fragrance

Egg-shaped buds open into exquisite, high-centered, pink blooms blushed with coral. Double, 3 to 4 inches, with 20 to 25 petals. Borne singly or in clusters. Light to moderate tea fragrance.

Form and Foliage

Medium-sized plant with a slightly spreading habit. Medium green, semiglossy foliage.

Peppermint Twist

ARS ___ Introduced 1992

Probably the best of the Jackson & Perkins Color Splash Series of floribundas. Flowers are striped with red, white and pink. Colorful landscape plant with good disease resistance. 'Purple Tiger', purple splashed with white and pink, is another in the series.

Flower and Fragrance

Pointed, ovoid buds open into large cupped blooms with red, pink and white stripes. Double, 4 inches, with 25 to 35 petals. Born in clusters. Slight fragrance.

Form and Foliage

Medium-sized, upright plant with medium green, semiglossy leaves.

Playboy

ARS 8.1 Introduced 1976

An eye-catching, single, orange-scarlet rose with bright gold eye. A fine landscape plant with excellent disease resistance. Hardy. Good cut flower.

Flower and Fragrance

Scarlet blooms with bright gold centers. Single, 3-1/2 inches, with 7 to 10 petals. Borne in large clusters. Slight fragrance.

Form and Foliage

Compact, upright plant with highly decorative, glossy, dark green foliage.

Pleasure

ARS 7.9 Introduced 1990, AARS 1990

The only rose to be designated an All-America Rose Selection for 1990, this free-blooming, salmon-colored floribunda deserves its name. Widely adapted and easy to grow, it makes an excellent hedge or border plant.

Flower and Fragrance

Pointed, ovoid buds open into flat salmon to coral blossoms. Double, 4 inches, with 30 to 35 petals. Slight fragrance.

Form and Foliage

Vigorous, upright plant with medium green foliage. Exceptional resistance to insect pests and hardy to winter cold.

■ ■ ■

Natural Garden Tip

A strong jet of water from a garden hose can help control many insects and diseases. A well-placed stream can knock aphids off new growth, keep undersides of leaves clean, reduce spider mites, and, according to some rose growers, wash off fungus spores, reducing infection from powdery mildew. Because wet foliage can encourage diseases such as rust and black spot, it's best to use this technique early in the morning so leaves can dry during the day.

■ ■ ■

Above: 'Rose Parade' is a free-blooming landscape rose. Its pink flowers are tinged with soft peach. Flowers are produced in clusters and have a strong fragrance.

Right: 'Razzle Dazzle' is a red and white bicolor. Flowers are hybrid tea-like, borne on compact plants.

Above left: 'Sexy Rexy'
flowers begin with clusters of
small pink buds, opening into
large sprays of 2- to 3-inch
blossoms. Also see photo on
page 85.

Above: 'Pleasure' was
awarded AARS status in
1990, the only rose that year
to receive that honor. It is
easy to grow, highly resistant
to insect pests and hardy to
cold.

Left: 'Sarabande' is a superior
landscape rose, particularly in
cool-summer regions.
Orange-red flowers are
profuse during summer,
covering the compact, low-
growing plant.

Razzle Dazzle   ARS 7.2 Introduced 1977

A bright, red and white bicolor with hybrid tea-like flowers borne on compact plants. Excellent cut flower.

Flower and Fragrance
Red buds open into large red blossoms with white reverse. Double, 3 to 4 inches, with 25 petals. Borne singly. Light fragrance.

Form and Foliage
Medium-sized, compact, upright plant with bright green leaves.

Redgold   ARS 7.4 Introduced 1971, AARS 1971

An intensely colored red and yellow rose. Best color develops with strong sunlight, cool temperatures. Good cut flower.

Flower and Fragrance
Bright yellow buds tipped with red open into golden yellow blossoms edged with scarlet-red. Double, 2-1/2 to 3 inches, with 25 to 30 petals. Borne singly or in clusters. Mild fruity fragrance.

Form and Foliage
Medium to tall, upright, bushy plant with medium green leaves.

Regensberg   ARS 8.5 Introduced 1975

A free-blooming, low-growing floribunda with large, white flowers splashed with pink. An excellent landscape or container plant, gaining in popularity. Largest flowers in cool weather. Accepts some shade.

Flower and Fragrance
Pink and white bicolor with bright yellow stamens. Semidouble, 4-1/2 inches, with 20 to 25 petals. Borne in clusters. Sweet apple fragrance.

Form and Foliage
Low-growing compact plant with glossy, dark green leaves. Makes a nice edging. Good disease resistance.

Rose Parade   ARS 7.0 Introduced 1974, AARS 1975

A pink rose with hints of soft peach. Flowers are nicely formed, a result of its 'Queen Elizabeth' heritage. A free-blooming landscape rose.

Flower and Fragrance
Large, ovoid buds open into large, cupped, pink blooms with a hint of coral-peach. Double, 3 to 3-1/2 inches, with 25 to 30 petals. Borne in clusters. Strong fragrance.

Form and Foliage
Vigorous, medium-sized, slightly spreading plant with dense, deep green foliage. Hardy and disease resistant.

Sarabande   ARS 8.0 Introduced 1959, AARS 1960

A favorite proven landscape rose with rich, orange-red flowers. Practically covers itself with blooms through the summer. Useful as low hedge, border or edging. Performs best in cool-summer climates but worth growing anywhere.

Flower and Fragrance
Deep, orangish red buds open into bright, scarlet-orange, cup-shaped flowers with sunny yellow stamens. Semidouble, 2-1/2 to 3 inches, with 10 to 15 petals. Borne in big clusters. Light, spicy fragrance.

Form and Foliage
Vigorous but compact, low-growing plant with medium green, semiglossy leaves. Good disease resistance and winter hardiness.

Saratoga   ARS 6.9 Introduced 1967, AARS 1968

A vigorous, free-blooming floribunda with white, very fragrant, gardenialike blossoms. Good disease resistance.

Flower and Fragrance
Ovoid buds open into large white blossoms. Double, 4 inches, with 30 to 35 petals. Borne in clusters. Very fragrant.

Form and Foliage
Upright, vigorous plant with glossy, deep green leaves.

Sea Pearl   ARS 7.8 Introduced 1964

A lovely, light pink rose with an apricot-yellow blush. Good cut flower. Widely adapted.

Flower and Fragrance
Large, pointed, pink buds open into soft pink blooms with apricot-yellow reverse. Double, 4-1/2 inches, with 25 petals. Borne singly and in clusters. Slight fragrance.

Form and Foliage
Vigorous, tall, upright plant with deep green leaves. Disease resistant and winter hardy.

Sexy Rexy   ARS 9.0 Introduced 1984

A prolific blooming, light pink, camellialike rose borne in huge clusters. Rapidly gaining in popularity. Good disease resistance. Fine cut flower. Excellent hedge or border plant.

Flower and Fragrance
Small pink buds open into large sprays of light pink blossoms. Double, 2 to 3 inches, with 40 petals. Slight fragrance.

Form and Foliage
Vigorous, medium-sized, bushy plant with light green leaves. Good disease resistance.

■ ■ ■

Natural Garden Tip

These pests can be reduced by spraying with horticultural oil:
Aphids
Caterpillars (some)
Mealy bugs
Mites
Scales
Whiteflies

These pests can be reduced by spraying insecticidal soap:
Aphids
Caterpillars (some)
Crickets
Earwigs
Grasshoppers
Leafhoppers
Mealy bugs
Mites
Sawflies (Rose slug)
Scales
Thrips

■ ■ ■

Above: 'Sweet Inspiration' was a 1993 AARS award winner. It is exceptionally free-blooming, and an excellent landscape rose.

Above right: 'Sunsprite' produces bright yellow flowers over a long season, making it excellent for use as a hedge or border.

Right: 'Showbiz' puts out large numbers of slightly fragrant, red flowers on a vigorous, compact plant, making it an exceptional landscape rose. Disease resistant.

Above and far left: 'Trumpeter', an easy-to-grow floribunda, is a repeat bloomer with good looks, well suited to landscape use. Orange-red, ruffled flowers are profuse, borne singly and in clusters.

Left: The lemon yellow flowers of 'Sun Flare' reach up to 3 inches wide and have a pleasing licorice scent.

Showbiz ARS 8.6 Introduced 1985, AARS 1985

Nonstop sprays of ruffled, fire-engine red blossoms on a low-growing, compact plant make this an exceptional landscape rose. Carefree and disease resistant.

Flower and Fragrance
Scarlet-red buds open into rich red, cup-shaped blossoms with slightly ruffled petals. Double, 2-1/2 to 3 inches, with 20 to 25 petals. Borne in clusters. Light fragrance.

Form and Foliage
Vigorous, compact, low-growing plant with glossy, dark green leaves.

Simplicity ARS 8.1 Introduced 1979

The most popular floribunda for landscape use. Free-blooming plant with a handsome, upright growth habit. Makes a superb hedge.

Flower and Fragrance
Slender, pointed buds open into bright pink, cup-shaped blossoms. Semidouble, 3 to 4 inches, with 18 to 20 petals. Borne in clusters. Little fragrance.

Form and Foliage
Vigorous, tall, upright plant with dense, deep green leaves. Good disease resistance and winter hardiness.

Singin' in the Rain ARS __ Introduced 1995, AARS 1995

Everchanging with the weather, this fine floribunda can range from apricot gold to rusty orange to even a cinnamon pink. Free-blooming and attractive landscape plant.

Flower and Fragrance
Well-formed pointed buds open into medium-sized blooms in shades of orange, apricot or cinnamon. Double, 3-1/2 inches, with 25 to 30 petals. Borne in clusters. Moderate musk fragrance.

Form and Foliage
Medium-sized, bushy plant with a round habit and glossy green foliage. Good disease resistance.

Sun Flare ARS 8.1 Introduced 1983, AARS 1983

A glowing, lemon yellow rose borne on a small, compact plant. Free-blooming. Superb landscape rose for border, edging or containers. Excellent disease resistance.

Flower and Fragrance
Pointed, bright yellow buds open into high-centered, lemon-yellow blossoms. Double, 3 inches, with 25 to 30 petals. Borne mostly in clusters. Light licorice scent.

Form and Foliage
Low-growing, slightly spreading plant with very glossy, deep green leaves.

Sunsprite

ARS 8.7 Introduced 1977

Bright yellow blossoms are borne over a long season. A handsome upright plant that makes a nice hedge.

Flower and Fragrance
Oval buds open into bright yellow, cup-shaped blooms. Double, 3 inches, with 25 to 30 petals. Borne in clusters. Strong fragrance.

Form and Foliage
Vigorous, medium-sized, upright plant with dark green, leathery leaves.

Sweet Inspiration

ARS ___ Introduced 1993, AARS 1993

An exceptionally free-blooming, pink floribunda that is an outstanding landscape rose. Covers itself with flowers. Good disease resistance.

Flower and Fragrance
High-centered buds open into large, soft pink blooms with a touch of cream at the base. Double, 4 inches, with 20 to 30 petals. Borne in large clusters. Slight fragrance.

Form and Foliage
Compact, mounded habit with medium green leaves.

The Fairy

ARS 8.7 Introduced 1941

Huge, arching clusters of small, coral-pink blooms highlight this excellent polyantha. Profuse blooming, easy to grow, hardy and disease resistant. Good as a border or ground cover or in mass plantings.

Flower and Fragrance
Coral-pink blossoms open into small, pastel pink blooms. Double, 1 to 1-1/2 inches, with 20 to 25 petals. Borne in large clusters. Mild, fruity fragrance.

Form and Foliage
Form is somewhat variable from upright to low and spreading. Small, shiny, light green leaves.

Trumpeter

ARS 8.3 Introduced 1977

Brilliant, orange-scarlet, ruffled blooms adorn this easy-to-grow floribunda. Excellent repeat bloom. Handsome form and foliage. Great landscape rose.

Flower and Fragrance
Ovoid buds open into glowing, orange-red blooms. Double, 2-1/2 to 3 inches, with 35 to 40 petals. Borne singly and in clusters. Mild fragrance.

Form and Foliage
Compact, low-growing plant with glossy, deep green foliage. Good disease resistance.

■ ■ ■
Natural Garden Tip

Soil solarization is a new, nontoxic technique used in hot, sunny climates to control soil-borne pests such as nematodes. It is most effective when done in midsummer. Water the planting area (it should be at least 6 by 9 feet) to a depth of at least 2 feet. Water again two days later. Cover the area with clear plastic that is at least 1 mil thick, and seal the edges securely with soil. Leave in place at least 6 weeks. The heat that builds up under the plastic is often enough to kill fungus and insect pests, as well as many weed seeds.

■ ■ ■

Grandifloras

The class of rose known as grandiflora was created as a home for a special garden rose named 'Queen Elizabeth', a hybrid of 'Floradora' and 'Charlotte Armstrong'. Most grandifloras, including 'Queen Elizabeth', produce an abundance of blossoms on full, clean-leaved plants—like their floribunda parents—but their clusters of flowers are the classic tea shape. Although 'Queen Elizabeth' and others are tall, upright plants to 6 feet high, newer introductions such as 'Tournament of Roses' are lower growing. Grandifloras are excellent landscape plants, often used as hedges, for screens or as a background, with good disease resistance and cold hardiness.

As popular as 'Queen Elizabeth' has become, the class grandiflora has not gained the popularity expected by its originators. This may be because many of the newer grandifloras are not as outstanding as 'Queen Elizabeth', varying in flower quality and growth habit. Consequently, European rose growers do not recognize grandiflora as a rose class. The American Rose Society has also considered dropping the classification. One grandiflora that does meet all expectations is 'Gold Medal'. It is an exceptional rose of wonderful substance and character. Recent introductions 'Tournament of Roses' and 'Prima Donna' appear as if they, too, are superior grandifloras, worthy of a place in the garden.

'Queen Elizabeth' is one of the most popular and commonly grown roses, and winner of almost every award imaginable. An abundant producer of clear pink flowers, it has many attributes: it's an excellent cut flower, useful hedge or background plant in the landscape, and is disease resistant and cold hardy.

Left: 'Gold Medal' is valued for its deep yellow flowers that retain their color and form.

Above: 'Love' is a productive bloomer, with hybrid tea-like flowers.

Below left: 'Prima Donna' flowers begin as long pointed buds and open into deep, long-stemmed, fuchsia-pink blooms.

Below: 'Tournament of Roses' was an AARS selection in 1989. An easy-to-grow plant.

Aquarius
ARS 8.0 Introduced 1971, AARS 1971

A large, pink blend with hybrid tea form. Easy to grow with excellent hardiness and disease resistance. Good cut flower.

Flower and Fragrance
Ovoid pink buds open into light pink, high-centered blossoms with petals edged in pink. Double, 3-1/2 to 4-1/2 inches, with 30 to 40 petals. Slight fragrance.

Form and Foliage
Full-foliaged, medium-sized, bushy plant with shiny, deep green leaves.

Arizona
ARS 5.8 Introduced 1975, AARS 1975

A blend of warm colors—golden orange and yellow with just a touch of pink. A handsome plant that makes a narrow, thorny hedge.

Flower and Fragrance
Ovoid buds open into nicely formed, bronzy yellow blossoms with hints of orange and pink. Double, 4 to 4-1/2 inches, with 35 to 40 petals. Strong, sweet fragrance.

Form and Foliage
Tall, upright, bushy plant with glossy, dark green, leathery leaves.

Camelot
ARS 7.3 Introduced 1964, AARS 1965

A salmon-pink rose that is more intensely colored in warm weather. A long-lasting cut flower. Densely foliaged plant makes a nice hedge. Best performance in the South.

Flower and Fragrance
Egg-shaped buds open into large, cup-shaped, salmon-pink blossoms. Double, 4-1/2 to 5 inches, with 45 to 50 petals. Light, spicy, clove fragrance.

Form and Foliage
Tall, vigorous and upright, with abundant, deep green, hollylike leaves. Disease resistant.

Caribbean
ARS ___ Introduced 1994, AARS 1994

A brilliant, bright orange rose with outstanding form and long stems ideal for cutting. Best color and form in cool, fall weather.

Flower and Fragrance
Pointed, oval buds swirl open into high-centered, bright orange blooms with yellow reverse. Double, 4 inches, with 30 to 35 petals. Slight fragrance.

Form and Foliage
Medium-sized, upright plant with semiglossy, dark green leaves. Good disease resistance but somewhat susceptible to mildew.

Carrousel
ARS 7.3 Introduced 1950

An easy-to-grow, prolific-blooming, deep red rose borne on a tall, stately plant. Useful as a hedge. Good disease resistance.

Flower and Fragrance
Deep red buds open into deep red blooms. Semidouble, 3 to 4 inches, with about 20 petals. Moderate, sweet fragrance.

Form and Foliage
Vigorous, tall, upright plant fully clothed in shiny, deep green leaves.

Gold Medal
ARS 8.8 Introduced 1983

Deep yellow blooms tipped with orange possess a consistent, shapely form. Performs best in the West; needs winter protection in coldest climates.

Flower and Fragrance
Shapely deep gold buds open into dark yellow blooms lightly touched with orange on the outer petals. Double, 3-1/2 inches, with 30 to 35 petals. Rich, fruity fragrance.

Form and Foliage
Tall, upright and bushy. Dark green, semiglossy leaves are prone to black spot.

Love
ARS 7.1 Introduced 1980, AARS 1980

A bicolored red rose with silvery white reverse. Very productive bloomer. Long-stemmed flowers have excellent, hybrid tea-like form. Good cut flower.

Flower and Fragrance
Pointed, silvery red buds open into star-shaped, bright red blossoms with silvery white reverse. Double, 3-1/2 inches, with 30 to 35 recurved petals. Slight spicy fragrance.

Form and Foliage
Does not grow as tall as most other grandifloras. Very thorny. Sparse leaves are medium green.

Montezuma
ARS 6.5 Introduced 1955

One of the oldest grandifloras, 'Montezuma' has withstood the test of time as a superior garden rose and cut flower. Prolific bloomer and easy to grow.

Flower and Fragrance
Urn-shaped, coral buds open into beautifully formed, salmon-pink blossoms, which become more coral-pink in cooler climates. Double, 3-1/2 to 4 inches, with 30 to 35 petals. Light tea fragrance.

Form and Foliage
Very vigorous, bushy, slightly spreading plant with leathery, deep green leaves.

■ ■ ■

Air-Drying Roses for Dried Flower Bouquets

Cut roses late in the afternoon. Strip leaves and thorns from bottom half of stem. Hang upside down in warm, well-ventilated area out of direct sun. A fan helps drying. After roses are dry (this usually takes at least one week), spray with plastic sealer, available in craft stores. Roses that are suitable subjects for air drying include:

Apricot Nectar
Brandy
Color Magic
Double Delight
Gold Medal
Ivory Tower
Las Vegas
Paradise
Prima Donna
Princesse de Monaco
Queen Elizabeth
Sea Pearl
Tournament of Roses

■ ■ ■

Olé

ARS 7.3 Introduced 1964

An interesting, orange-red Spanish rose with crinkly, ruffled petals. A generous bloomer with attractive, dark green leaves.

Flower and Fragrance

Nicely shaped buds open into cup-shaped, orange-red blossoms with ruffled petals. Double, 3-1/2 to 4 inches, with 40 to 45 petals. Slight fruity fragrance.

Form and Foliage

Bushy, medium-sized plant is disease resistant, with shiny, dark green leaves.

Prima Donna

ARS 7.5 Introduced 1988, AARS 1988

A stunning, fuchsia-pink rose borne on a vigorous, free-blooming plant. Makes an elegant cut flower.

Flower and Fragrance

Long, pointed buds swirl open into deep, fuchsia-pink blooms. Double, 4 inches, with 25 petals. Mild tea fragrance.

Form and Foliage

Tall, upright plant with semiglossy green leaves. Tends to be susceptible to mildew and black spot. Lacks winter hardiness.

Prominent

ARS 7.2 Introduced 1971, AARS 1977

A small, bright orange-red rose prized as a long-lasting cut flower. Blooms over a long season.

Flower and Fragrance

Ovoid buds open into star-shaped to cupped, orange-red blossoms with recurved petals. Double, 2-1/2 to 3-1/2 inches, with 25 to 30 petals. Light fruity fragrance.

Form and Foliage

Tall, upright, well-branched plant with dull green leaves. Good winter hardiness.

Queen Elizabeth

ARS 9.0 Introduced 1954, AARS 1955

One of the finest and most popular roses. Winner of almost every award. Tall and stately with dense, deep green leaves and an abundance of clear pink flowers. Useful as a hedge or background plant. Excellent cut flower.

Flower and Fragrance

Pointed, deep pink buds open into high-centered to cupped pink blossoms. Double, 3-1/2 to 4 inches, with 35 to 40 petals. Moderate tea fragrance.

Form and Foliage

Tall, very vigorous growth and dense foliage. Leaves are dark green, glossy and leathery. Disease resistant. Good winter hardiness.

Shining Hour
ARS 7.6 Introduced 1991, AARS 1991

A bright yellow rose held stately against a dense, clean-foliaged plant. Free-blooming. Good cut flower. Best performance in the West.

Flower and Fragrance
Pointed, egg-shaped buds open into bright yellow blooms. Double, 4 inches, with 35 petals. Lightly sweet fragrance.

Form and Foliage
Upright, dense plant with medium green leaves. Good disease resistance.

Shreveport
ARS 6.7 Introduced 1982, AARS 1982

Named for the home of the American Rose Society. A lush, bushy plant with notable disease resistance and hardiness.

Flower and Fragrance
Shapely orange buds open into high-centered blossoms in shades of orange, yellow and coral. Double, 3-1/2 to 4 inches, with 45 to 50 petals. Mild tea fragrance.

Form and Foliage
Tall, upright plant with an abundance of glossy, deep green leaves.

Solitude
ARS ___ Introduced 1993, AARS 1993

Touched with the colors of the sunset, this fine grandiflora has bright orange flowers with orange-gold reverse. Compact, bushy plant with above-average disease resistance. Colors more intense in hot weather.

Flower and Fragrance
High-centered, oval buds open into bright orange blooms with touches of yellow and gold. Double, 4 to 5 inches, with 30 to 35 petals. Light spicy fragrance.

Form and Foliage
Upright, bushy plant with rich green foliage.

Sonia
ARS 8.1 Introduced 1974

The long, tapered buds of this coral-pink rose have made it a favorite of florists, exhibitors and lovers of cut flowers.

Flower and Fragrance
Perfectly formed, elongated pink buds open into high-centered, pink flowers suffused with coral and yellow. Double, 3-1/2 to 4 inches, with 25 to 30 petals. Sweet, fruity fragrance.

Form and Foliage
Medium-sized, bushy plant with deep green, glossy foliage.

Spellcaster
ARS ___ Introduced 1991

An unusually colored rose with heavily textured lavender blooms. Borne on a dense, bushy plant. Good cut flower.

Flower and Fragrance
Pointed, oval buds open into deep lavender blooms with petal edges touched with red. Double, 4 inches, with 35 to 40 petals. Moderate fragrance.

Form and Foliage
Upright, dense plant with glossy, dark green foliage.

Sundowner
ARS 6.0 Introduced 1978, AARS 1979

A reliable producer of hybrid tea-like flowers in sunset shades of orange and salmon-pink. Good cut flower.

Flower and Fragrance
Nicely shaped, apricot-orange buds open into large, golden orange blooms tinted with salmon. Double, 3-1/2 to 4 inches, with 35 to 40 petals. Powerful, spicy fragrance.

Form and Foliage
Vigorous, tall and upright with glossy, deep green leaves.

Tournament of Roses
ARS 8.0 Introduced 1988, AARS 1989

A coral-pink rose named to honor the 100th anniversary of the Pasadena Tournament of Roses. An easy-to-grow, free-blooming, handsome plant adapted to a wide range of climates. Good disease resistance.

Flower and Fragrance
Deep, coral-pink buds spiral open into high-centered, coral-pink blossoms that gradually soften to light pink. Double, 4 inches, with 25 to 30 petals. Light spicy fragrance.

Form and Foliage
Medium-sized, bushy, upright plant with glossy, deep green leaves.

White Lightnin'
ARS 6.6 Introduced 1980, AARS 1981

A wonderful, crystal white rose with a strong, lemony fragrance. Very handsome, compact plant. Good cut flower.

Flower and Fragrance
Slender pointed buds open into clean white blossoms with ruffled petals that are sometimes lightly dusted with pink. Double, 3-1/2 to 4 inches, with 30 to 35 petals. Strong citrus scent.

Form and Foliage
Compact, rounded bush clothed in glossy, deep green leaves.

■ ■ ■

Grandifloras with Fragrance

Arizona
Gold Medal
Sonia
Sundowner
White Lightnin'

■ ■ ■

Miniatures

Miniatures are the lilliputians of the rose world. Smaller in stature but not in beauty, they continue to gain in popularity each year. Their flowers possess all the perfection and substance of a hybrid tea, and plants can be as colorful and useful in the landscape as the best floribunda. Despite their delicate appearance, miniatures are not difficult to grow, and have the same cultural requirements as other roses.

Miniature roses range in height from 6 inches to 3 feet. Most grow 1 to 1-1/2 feet high. Flowers are borne on short, wiry stems, usually in great profusion from spring until fall. In the landscape, miniatures make wonderful, colorful edgings, especially along walkways. They are exceptional container plants. Miniature roses can also be used as low hedges, borders or mass plantings.

Some gardeners grow miniature roses indoors, although this is not a common practice for beginners. At the very least, plants need a bright, sunny, south-facing window to attain bloom. For best results, supplemental artificial lights should be provided.

Many varieties of miniature roses are available, with specialists such as Ralph Moore at Sequoia Nursery adding a wealth of new varieties each year. Miniatures judged outstanding at test gardens throughout the United States receive the American Rose Society Award of Excellence.

Opposite: Due to their stature and profuse flowers, miniatures are natural choices for containers. These roses are on display at Pixie Treasures, a grower-retailer in Southern California.

Left: A rose gardener in the market for miniatures takes advantage of the miniatures display at Portland International Rose Garden in Portland, Oregon.

Below left: When growing several miniatures in containers, a drip-irrigation system is an effective and efficient method of watering plants.

Below: 'Starina' is one of the highest rated of all miniature roses, prized for its flower form and plant growth habit. It is used both as a cut flower and versatile landscape plant.

Acey Deucy   ARS 8.3 Introduced 1982

A bright red miniature with small but beautiful, hybrid tea-like blossoms. Plant in containers or as an edging.

Flower and Fragrance
Small red buds open into high-centered, red blossoms. Double, 1 to 2 inches, with 20 petals. Slight fragrance.

Form and Foliage
Medium-sized, bushy plant with small, medium green leaves.

Baby Betsy McCall   ARS 7.9 Introduced 1960

A compact, low-growing miniature with light pink flowers. Good repeat bloom. Makes a fine edging or container plant.

Flower and Fragrance
Small pink buds open into cup-shaped, light pink blossoms. Double, 1 to 1-1/2 inches, with 20 to 25 petals. Fragrant.

Form and Foliage
Small, compact plant with dense, leathery green leaves.

Beauty Secret   ARS 8.4 Introduced 1965

A beautiful, sweetly fragrant miniature, and winner of the ARS Award of Excellence in 1975. Fine edging or low border. Excellent container plant.

Flower and Fragrance
Nicely shaped, pointed buds open into medium red blooms with hybrid-tea form. Double, 1 to 1-1/2 inches, with 25 to 30 petals. Strong fragrance.

Form and Foliage
Compact, medium to tall and upright with good vigor. Small, shiny green leaves. Disease resistant and hardy.

Billie Teas   ARS ___ Introduced 1992

Winner of ARS Award of Excellence in 1993. Deep red, full-petaled blossoms are borne singly.

Flower and Fragrance
Beautifully formed, deep red flowers. Double, 1 to 2 inches, with 25 to 40 petals. Little fragrance.

Form and Foliage
Medium-sized, upright miniature with dull green leaves.

Black Jade
ARS 7.1 Introduced 1985

Unique flowering miniature with blackish red buds opening into the deepest red blossoms. Long-stemmed cut flower. Good disease resistance but can get mildew. Received ARS Award of Excellence in 1985.

Flower and Fragrance
Blackish red buds open into deep red blooms. Double, 2 inches, with 25 to 30 petals. Slight fragrance.

Form and Foliage
Upright, rounded growth with glossy, dark green leaves.

Bojangles
ARS 6.6 Introduced 1983

An excellent lemon yellow landscape rose, producing an abundance of brightly colored flowers over a long season. Ideal as an edging or low border or in containers.

Flower and Fragrance
Small buds open into deep yellow blossoms. Double, 1-1/2 to 2 inches, with 20 petals. Little fragrance.

Form and Foliage
Vigorous, compact plant with small, glossy, light green leaves. Disease resistant and winter hardy.

Cal Poly
ARS ___ Introduced 1992

An exceptionally free-blooming, long-lasting yellow miniature. Summer heat improves the character of the flowers. Awarded ARS Award of Excellence in 1992.

Flower and Fragrance
Bright yellow blossoms borne in clusters. Double, 2 to 3 inches, with 25 to 30 petals. Slight fragrance.

Form and Foliage
Small to medium, mounded plant with semiglossy green leaves.

Center Gold
ARS 6.9 Introduced 1981

A vigorous, upright plant with golden yellow flowers. Prolific bloomer. Good border plant. Winner of ARS Award of Excellence in 1982.

Flower and Fragrance
Nicely shaped, pointed buds swirl open into hybrid tea-like, golden yellow blossoms. Double, 1-1/2 inches, with 25 to 35 petals. Spicy fragrance.

Form and Foliage
Tall, vigorous, upright plant with shiny, medium green leaves. Disease resistant and cold hardy.

Above: 'Cinderella' is a time-honored miniature, introduced in 1953. It's a vigorous, low-growing, compact plant, producing abundant, light pink to white fragrant flowers.

Above right: 'Center Gold' produces a smaller version of hybrid tea flowers in shades of golden yellow. The tall, upright plant is disease resistant and cold hardy.

Right: Miniatures are excellent edging plants in the landscape. Here, the pinkish red flowers of 'Child's Play' complement the flowers of a large, weeping 'Margo Koster', a polyantha.

Above left: 'Cuddles' is an easy-to-grow miniature with deep, coral-pink flowers. The low-growing, bushy plant is disease resistant and hardy.

Above: 'Cupcake' produces hybrid tea-like flowers that are 1-1/2 inches across. It's a reliable, repeat-blooming miniature.

Left: 'Debut', along with 'New Beginnings', was the first miniature to be awarded AARS honors. The abundant flowers are double, 2 inches across, in a rich red touched with white at the base. The handsome, medium-sized plant is disease resistant.

Child's Play   ARS ___ Introduced 1993, AARS 1993

An easy-to-grow, vigorous plant with white blossoms edged with pinkish red. Fine landscape plant with a low-growing compact habit. Best color in warm summer climates.

Flower and Fragrance

Pointed buds open into white flowers edged with pinkish red. Double, 1-1/2 to 2 inches, with 20 petals. Flowers borne mostly singly. Light, sweet fragrance.

Form and Foliage

Low-growing, mounding plant with large, medium green leaves.

Cinderella   ARS 8.0 Introduced 1953

One of the finest and most popular miniatures. Low-growing, compact plant produces an abundance of light pink to white, fragrant flowers. Excellent edging or container plant.

Flower and Fragrance

Oval buds open into pale pink, cup-shaped blossoms that fade to white. Double, 1/2 to 1 inch, with 45 to 55 petals. Strong, spicy fragrance is exceptional for a miniature.

Form and Foliage

Small, compact, slightly spreading plant with small, glossy green leaves. Good disease resistance.

Cloud Nine   ARS 6.0 Introduced 1984

Snow-white blossoms are produced in abundance on a compact, handsome plant. Fine choice for landscaping, as an edging or container plant.

Flower and Fragrance

Small white buds open into clean white blossoms. Semidouble, 1-1/2 inches, with 15 to 20 petals. Little fragrance.

Form and Foliage

Compact, slightly spreading plant, with light green leaves. Disease resistant and winter hardy.

Cuddles   ARS 7.7 Introduced 1978

An easy-to-grow, versatile miniature with deep, coral-pink flowers. Free-blooming. Useful as an edging or in containers. Winner of ARS Award of Excellence in 1979.

Flower and Fragrance

Oval buds unfurl into hybrid tea-like, coral-pink blooms with recurved petals. Double, 1 to 1-1/2 inches, with 55 to 60 petals. Slight fragrance.

Form and Foliage

Low-growing, bushy plant with shiny, medium green leaves. Disease resistant and hardy.

Cupcake
ARS 8.5 Introduced 1981

A reliable, clear pink rose. Good repeat bloom of full-petaled, hybrid tea-like flowers.

Flower and Fragrance
Pointed pink buds swirl open into high-centered pink blossoms. Double, 1-1/2 inches, with 50 petals. Little fragrance.

Form and Foliage
Vigorous, bushy, medium-sized plant with glossy green leaves.

Debut
ARS 7.4 Introduced 1989, AARS 1989

Along with 'New Beginnings', the first miniature to be awarded AARS honors. Abundant, deep red blooms are touched with ivory-white at the base and are borne in profusion.

Flower and Fragrance
Small, pointed buds swirl open into rich, deep red blooms with silvery white shadings at base of petals. Double, 2 inches, with 15 to 20 petals. Slight fragrance.

Form and Foliage
Handsome, medium-sized, compact, rounded plant with shiny, deep green leaves. Good disease resistance.

Dreamglo
ARS 8.5 Introduced 1978

A multipetaled, red and white blended rose with classic, hybrid tea form. Fine landscape rose. Good repeat bloom.

Flower and Fragrance
Small, pointed buds open into red, high-centered blooms that blend with white at the base of petals. Double, 1 inch, with 50 petals. Light fragrance.

Form and Foliage
Tall, upright, well-branched plant with semiglossy, dark green leaves. Disease resistant and cold hardy.

Figurine
ARS ___ Introduced 1992

A classically formed flower in ivory tinged with pink. Free-blooming. Good for cut flowers. Nice edging plant.

Flower and Fragrance
Well-formed, very light pink buds open into ivory flowers with just a tinge of pink. Double, 1 to 2 inches, with 15 to 25 petals. Pleasant light fragrance.

Form and Foliage
Medium-sized, bushy plant with deep green leaves.

Right: 'Holy Toledo' is a bicolor miniature with apricot-orange and yellow flowers. The medium-to-tall plant is vigorous, disease resistant and hardy.

Below: 'Lavender Jewel' is often considered to be the top choice for a lavender-flowering miniature. Its long season of bloom makes it a fine choice for containers or hanging baskets.

Below right: 'Funny Girl' is a small, compact plant—usually reaching no more than 1 foot high. It is well suited to narrow planting spots.

Above: Among a hillside planting of roses, the bright white flowers of 'Gourmet Popcorn' help guide the way along a path. This popular miniature is a good repeat bloomer.

Left: 'Judy Fischer' is a free-flowering miniature often used for cutting. Flowers are small, just 1/2 to 1 inch wide, with a slight fragrance. Plant is low-growing and compact, useful in the landscape.

Funny Girl   ARS 6.7 Introduced 1983

A beautiful crystal pink rose borne on a very small, compact plant that rarely
exceeds a foot high. An exceptional landscape plant for narrow areas. Also good
in containers.

Flower and Fragrance
Tiny pink buds open into clear pink blossoms. Double, 1-1/2 inches, with 20
petals. Slight fragrance.

Form and Foliage
Small, very compact plant with medium green leaves. Good disease resistance
and winter hardiness.

Gourmet Popcorn   ARS 8.4 Introduced 1986

Bright white, single flowers with buttery yellow stamens give this popular
miniature its name. Good repeat bloom. Excellent disease-resistant landscape
plant. 'Popcorn' is similar but has smaller flowers.

Flower and Fragrance
Slender white buds open into creamy white blossoms with bright yellow
stamens. Double, 1 inch, with 18 to 20 petals. Strong fragrance.

Form and Foliage
Vigorous, slightly spreading plant with clean looking, dark green leaves.

Heavenly Days   ARS 7.6 Introduced 1988

A brightly colored, ever-changing miniature in blended shades of orange, yellow,
red and pink. Winner of the 1988 Award of Excellence. Fine landscape plant.

Flower and Foliage
Small, shapely buds open into orange, cup-shaped blossoms with yellow reverse.
As blooms age, the color changes from orange to red and pink. Double, 1-1/2 to 2
inches, with 28 to 32 petals. No fragrance.

Form and Foliage
Vigorous, compact, bushy plant with glossy, medium green leaves.

Holy Toledo   ARS 7.9 Introduced 1978

A consistent-blooming bicolor rose consisting of apricot-orange and yellow.
Good repeat bloomer. Winner of ARS Award of Excellence in 1980.

Flower and Fragrance
Shapely buds open into colorful, dark apricot blossoms with yellow base and
reverse. Double, 1-1/2 to 2 inches, with 25 to 30 petals. Slight fragrance.

Form and Foliage
Medium to tall plant with shiny, dark green leaves. Vigorous, disease resistant
and hardy.

Judy Fischer

ARS 7.8 Introduced 1968

A free-flowering, long-lasting, pink miniature that won an ARS Award of Excellence in 1975. Good cut flower.

Flower and Fragrance
Nicely shaped, pointed buds open into rose-pink blossoms. Double, 1/2 to 1 inch, with 20 to 25 petals. Slight fragrance.

Form and Foliage
Low-growing, compact plant with shiny, dark green leaves. Disease resistant.

Kathy

ARS 7.4 Introduced 1970

A red rose with hints of orange borne on a low, spreading plant. Ideal for edging, containers or hanging baskets. Good repeat bloom.

Flower and Fragrance
Small, pointed buds open into red blooms that have a slight suggestion of orange. Double, 1-1/2 inches, with 25 to 30 petals. Moderate fragrance.

Form and Foliage
Low-growing, spreading, compact plant with dark green, semiglossy leaves. Disease resistant and hardy.

Kathy Robinson

ARS 7.9 Introduced 1968

A longtime favorite pink rose with cream reverse. Profuse bloomer throughout the season. Good landscape rose.

Flower and Fragrance
Pointed buds open into high-centered, blended pink blossoms with cream reverse. Double, 1 to 1-1/2 inches, with 25 to 30 petals. Slight fragrance.

Form and Foliage
Medium-sized, compact, bushy plant with shiny, medium green leaves. Disease resistant and hardy.

Lavender Jewel

ARS 7.5 Introduced 1978

Considered by many to be the finest lavender miniature, 'Lavender Jewel' is an excellent container plant that can also be grown in hanging baskets. Long season of bloom.

Flower and Fragrance.
Small, pointed buds open into soft, lilac-purple, cup-shaped blossoms. Double, 1 to 1-1/2 inches, with 35 to 40 petals. Slight fragrance.

Form and Foliage
Small to medium, compact plant with glossy, dark green leaves. Good disease resistance.

■ ■ ■

Natural Garden Tip

Floating row covers are partially transparent, blanketlike products, often used to protect vegetable crops from insect pests. They can also be used as barriers to exclude certain pests from roses. Low-growing miniatures, roses in containers or prized specimens are good candidates for row cover protection. Cover plants when insects such as Japanese beetles or borers are at peak activity, sealing the edges with soil, to keep the pests out.

■ ■ ■

Above: 'Pride 'n Joy' is a fine landscape plant, useful for borders, edgings and containers. Its bright orange flowers are hybrid tea-like in form, reaching 1 to 1-1/2 inches across.

Above right: 'Puppy Love' is a free-blooming miniature producing multicolored flowers. Winner of the ARS Award of Excellence in 1979.

Right: 'New Beginnings' was one of first two miniatures to receive AARS status. (See 'Debut', page 123.) The 2-inch flowers are hot orange with yellow reverse. Use as an edging or low hedge or in containers.

Little Artist
ARS 8.5 Introduced 1982

A lovely, bicolored miniature bearing bright red flowers with white eyes and reverse. Long-lasting flowers. Excellent disease resistance.

Flower and Fragrance
Red buds open into red flowers with white centers, bright yellow stamens and white reverse. Semidouble, 1 inch, with 10 to 15 petals. Light fragrance.

Form and Foliage
Rounded, medium-sized plant with shiny green leaves.

Magic Carrousel
ARS 9.0 Introduced 1972

A colorful, much-loved miniature with red flowers edged with white. Winner of the ARS Award of Excellence in 1975. Continuous, long-lasting bloom. Good cut flower. Easy to grow.

Flower and Fragrance
Small, pointed buds open into red, cup-shaped blossoms edged with white. Double, 1-1/2 to 2 inches, with about 20 petals. Light fragrance.

Form and Foliage
Tall, vigorous plant is densely clothed in glossy, medium green leaves. Disease resistant and hardy.

Mary Marshall
ARS 8.0 Introduced 1970

A popular coral-orange and yellow miniature known for its generous bloom and well-shaped flowers. Winner of ARS Award of Excellence in 1975. Fine cut flower.

Flower and Fragrance
Pointed buds swirl open into hybrid tea-like, coral-orange blooms with yellow base. Double, 1-1/2 inches, with 25 to 30 petals. Slight fragrance.

Form and Foliage
Medium-sized, upright plant well clothed in medium green, leathery leaves. Climbing form available. Good disease resistance.

New Beginnings
ARS 7.1 Introduced 1989, AARS 1989

Along with 'Debut', the first miniature to achieve AARS. The hot orange blossoms have a yellow reverse. Easy-to-grow, compact plant makes an excellent edging, low hedge or container subject. Good repeat bloom.

Flower and Fragrance
Beautifully formed buds open into high-centered, bright orange-red blossoms with yellow reverse. Double, 1-1/2 to 2 inches, with 40 to 50 petals. Slight fragrance.

Form and Foliage
Medium to tall plant with neat, compact, rounded habit and dark green leaves. Good disease resistance.

Old Glory
ARS 7.8 Introduced 1988

A recipient of the 1988 Award of Excellence, this is an exceptional miniature with deep red, beautifully shaped flowers. Use as a colorful edging or low border or in containers.

Flower and Fragrance
Small but beautifully shaped buds open into deep red, hybrid tea-like blossoms. Double, 1-1/2 to 2 inches, with 23 to 25 petals. No fragrance.

Form and Foliage
Tall, vigorous, upright plant with semiglossy, medium green leaves.

Over the Rainbow
ARS 8.3 Introduced 1974

A bright red, pink and golden yellow rose. Winner of the ARS Award of Excellence in 1975. Good repeat bloom. Also available in a climbing form.

Flower and Fragrance
Nicely formed buds open into red and pink blossoms with golden yellow centers and reverse. Double, 1 to 1-1/2 inches, with 25 to 35 petals. Little or no fragrance.

Form and Foliage
Low-growing, bushy plant with dark green leaves. Climbing form can reach 5 to 6 feet high. Disease resistant and hardy.

Party Girl
ARS 9.0 Introduced 1979

A sweetly fragrant, apricot-yellow and salmon-pink blend that makes a fine landscape or container plant. Winner of ARS Award of Merit in 1981.

Flower and Fragrance
Shapely pointed buds open into high-centered, apricot-yellow blooms touched with salmon-pink. Double, 1 to 1-1/2 inches, with 25 petals. Strong, spicy fragrance.

Form and Foliage
Small to medium-sized, bushy plant with shiny, dark green leaves. Disease resistant and cold hardy.

Peaches 'n' Cream
ARS 8.4 Introduced 1976

Aptly named, this peach-pink and cream blend makes a lovely edging and a fine cut flower. Winner of the ARS Award of Excellence in 1977.

Flower and Fragrance
Pointed buds open into shapely, orange-pink blooms touched with cream. Double, 1 to 1-1/2 inches, with 50 to 55 petals. Slight fragrance.

Form and Foliage
Small to medium-sized plant that is slightly spreading. Shiny, dark green leaves. Disease resistant and hardy.

Pride 'n' Joy

ARS ___ Introduced 1992, AARS 1992

Bright orange blooms with yellow reverse have hybrid tea-like form. Fine landscape plant for edgings, low borders or containers. Good disease resistance.

Flower and Fragrance
Pointed buds open into orange blooms with yellow on the backs of the petals. Double, 1 to 1-1/2 inches, with 20 to 25 petals. Little fragrance.

Form and Foliage
Medium-sized, mounding plant with matte green leaves.

Puppy Love

ARS 7.4 Introduced 1978

A free-blooming, colorful miniature that won the ARS Award of Excellence in 1979.

Flower and Fragrance
Shapely, pointed buds swirl open into multicolored blooms of orange, pink and yellow. Double, 1-1/2 inches, with 20 to 25 petals. Slight fragrance.

Form and Foliage
Medium-sized, upright and bushy with medium green leaves.

Rainbow's End

ARS 9.0 Introduced 1986

A stunningly colorful yellow miniature with petals edged red. Winner of the Award of Excellence in 1986. A fine container plant. Good disease resistance.

Flower and Fragrance
Small buds open into clear yellow blossoms with petals edged in red, fading entirely to red. Double, 1-1/2 to 2 inches, with 35 petals. No fragrance.

Form and Foliage
Upright, bushy plant with glossy, dark green leaves.

Red Cascade

ARS 7.2 Introduced 1976

A consistent-blooming climbing miniature that is excellent for landscape use. Can be grown as a ground cover, in hanging baskets or to climb up just about anything. Won the ARS Award of Excellence in 1976.

Flower and Fragrance
Small buds open into deep red, cup-shaped blossoms. Double, 1 to 1-1/2 inches, with 35 to 40 petals. Light fragrance.

Form and Foliage
Spreading plant with arching canes that reach 4 to 6 feet long. Dense, dark green leaves tend to mildew.

■ ■ ■

Natural Garden Tip

If you're considering including beneficial insects in your pest control program, a free copy of *Suppliers of Beneficial Organisms in North America* is available from California Environmental Protection Agency, Department of Pesticide Regulation, Environmental Monitoring and Pest Management
1020 N Street
Room 161
Sacramento, Calif. 95814.

■ ■ ■

Rise 'n' Shine

ARS 9.1 Introduced 1977

One of the best yellow miniatures, prized for its long bloom season and attractive growth habit. Excellent landscape rose. Won ARS Award of Merit in 1978.

Flower and Fragrance
Beautifully shaped buds open into high-centered, bright yellow blooms. Double, 1-1/2 inches, with 35 to 40 petals. Slight fragrance.

Form and Foliage
Low-growing, compact, mound-shaped plant with dark green leaves.

Rosmarin

ARS 7.8 Introduced 1965

A strong-growing, reliable miniature with blush pink and red blended flowers. Known for its exceptional hardiness and consistent bloom. Good for edgings and low borders.

Flower and Fragrance
Globular pink buds open into full, cup-shaped, light pink blooms with red edges. Double, 1-1/2 inches, with 35 petals. Moderate fragrance.

Form and Foliage
Vigorous, medium to tall, upright habit. Shiny, medium green leaves.

Sequoia Gold

ARS 7.1 Introduced 1987

A 1987 Award of Excellence winner renowned for its profuse bloom and ability to hold its bright yellow color even in the hottest weather. A high-quality landscape plant for edging or containers.

Flower and Fragrance
Small yellow buds open into sunny yellow blooms. Double, 1 to 2 inches, with 20 to 25 petals. Little fragrance.

Form and Foliage
Vigorous, slightly spreading plant with deep green leaves. Good disease resistance.

Sheri Anne

ARS 7.6 Introduced 1973

A reliable producer of orange-red blooms on a compact bush. ARS Award of Excellence in 1975. Good cut flower.

Flower and Fragrance
Pointed buds open into showy, orange-red blossoms. Semidouble, 1 to 1-1/2 inches, with 15 to 18 petals. Little fragrance.

Form and Foliage
Medium to tall, upright, well-branched plant with glossy, dark green leaves.

Left: 'Starina', like most miniatures, is an appealing subject for containers. Its hybrid tea-like flowers reach to 2 inches across and have a slight fragrance. Also see photo, page 117.

Below left: 'Rise 'n' Shine' is at the top of the list for yellow-flowering miniatures. Its long season of bloom and low-growing, compact habit make it a useful landscape subject.

Below: 'Sheri Anne' is a reliable performer with semidouble orange-red blooms. Winner of ARS Award of Excellence in 1975.

Simplex   ARS 8.2 Introduced 1961

A proven, popular rose, this single white miniature is a fine border and container
plant. Flowers pick up a pink blush in cool, cloudy weather. Free-blooming.

Flower and Fragrance
Pointed, soft apricot buds open into flat, white blossoms with yellow stamens.
Single, 1 to 1-1/2 inches, with 5 petals. Slight fragrance.

Form and Foliage
Vigorous, bushy, medium-to-tall plant with leathery leaves.

Snow Bride   ARS 9.3 Introduced 1982

Perfectly formed white flowers make this a prize exhibition rose. Good cut
flower. ARS Award of Excellence in 1982.

Flower and Fragrance
Beautifully formed white buds open into formal white blossoms. Double, 1-1/2
to 2-1/2 inches, with 20 to 25 petals. Mild fragrance.

Form and Foliage
Small to medium-sized, bushy plant with deep green leaves.

Starglo   ARS 7.9 Introduced 1973

A surprisingly fragrant miniature with white flowers. Fine landscape plant.
Winner of ARS Award of Merit in 1975.

Flower and Fragrance
Long, pointed buds open into high-centered, white blossoms. Double, 1-1/2 to 2
inches, with 35 petals. Strong fragrance.

Form and Foliage
Small to medium-sized, bushy plant with shiny, medium green leaves.

Starina   ARS 9.0 Introduced 1965

Near perfection in flower form and plant habit have made 'Starina' one of the
most popular miniatures. A recipient of many awards. Possesses one of the
highest ARS ratings of any rose. Good repeat bloom. Excellent cut flower and
landscape plant.

Flower and Fragrance
Exquisitely formed, hybrid tea-like buds swirl open into perfectly shaped,
glowing, orange-red blossoms. Double, 1-1/2 to 2 inches, with 35 petals. Slight
fragrance.

Form and Foliage
Small to medium-sized, compact plant with dense, glossy green leaves. Disease
resistant and hardy.

Toy Clown
ARS 8.1 Introduced 1966

A free-blooming, bicolored miniature ideally suited to containers, either indoors or out. Also makes a colorful edging. Multiple award winner.

Flower and Fragrance
Long, pointed buds open into cup-shaped, red blossoms edged with white. Semidouble, 1-1/2 inches, with 15 to 20 petals. Slight fragrance.

Form and Foliage
Medium-sized, mound-shaped plant with small, medium green leaves.

Yellow Doll
ARS 7.2 Introduced 1962

A long-popular, free-blooming, light yellow miniature proven to be easy to grow. Plant is low growing and smallish, making an ideal edging or container plant.

Flower and Fragrance
Pointed yellow buds slowly unfurl into high-centered, sunny yellow blossoms. Double, 1-1/2 inches, with 50 to 60 petals. Moderate fragrance.

Form and Foliage
Small, compact plant with vigorous growth. Deep green leaves. Disease resistant and hardy.

Winsome
ARS 8.5 Introduced 1984

An alluring, deep purplish to lavender-red rose. Free-blooming, disease-resistant plant. ARS Award of Excellence in 1985.

Flower and Fragrance
Large, pointed buds open into full lavender-purple blooms. Double, 1-1/2 to 2-1/2 inches, with 35 to 40 petals. Little fragrance.

Form and Foliage
Vigorous, bushy plant with rounded habit and dark green leaves.

■ ■ ■

Disease-Resistant Miniatures

Black Jade
Child's Play
Debut
Holy Toledo
Magic Carrousel
Mary Marshall
New Beginnings
Sequoia Gold
Starina
Winsome
Yellow Doll

■ ■ ■

Climbing Roses

Climbing roses can be divided into two basic classes: large-flowering climbers and climbing sports. Large-flowering climbers, the most popular, are profuse bloomers. Their vigorous plants produce stiff canes that reach 6 to 20 feet high. Most bear beautiful clusters of flowers over a long season and are versatile, appealing landscape plants. Some of the less vigorous, large-flowering climbers are often referred to as pillar roses. The majority of the roses described in this chapter are large-flowering climbers.

Climbing sports are variations or mutants of popular forms that include hybrid teas, floribundas, grandifloras and other roses. You can purchase such well-known roses as 'Climbing Charlotte Armstrong', 'Climbing First Prize', 'Climbing Iceberg', 'Climbing Chrysler Imperial', 'Climbing Peace', 'Climbing Sutter's Gold' and dozens of others. Their flowers are very similar to their namesakes but are seldom as free-flowering. In the rose descriptions in this book, it is noted if a climbing sport of that rose is widely available. In general, when allotting space for climbing sports, figure that most produce canes that grow 8 to 15 feet high.

In the landscape, climbing roses are uniquely useful plants. However, to call them climbing roses is a bit of a misnomer: None actually climbs or clings as many vines do. Instead, the stiff canes must be tied to some kind of support. But therein lies their usefulness. Climbing roses are easy to train and sprawl over an arbor, snake along a fence or fan across a trellis. Wherever you can provide a sturdy support, you can train a climbing rose to grow on it.

Left: 'Dortmund' is a striking, single-flowering climber, producing large clusters of bright red flowers with white centers.

Opposite: Nothing is more dramatic in the garden than a red-flowering climber in full bloom.

Altissimo   ARS 9.3 Introduced 1967

This is a stunning imported rose that is gaining in popularity. The flowers are
huge, single and striking blood red. They are wonderful as cut flowers. Plant is
vigorous, free-blooming and basically problem-free.

Flower and Fragrance
Large pointed buds open into deep red, cup-shaped blossoms with yellow
stamens. Single, 4 to 5 inches, with 5 to 7 petals. Borne in clusters. Slight
fragrance.

Form and Foliage
Tall, vigorous grower with deep green, serrated leaves. Good disease resistance.

America   ARS 8.8 Introduced 1976, AARS 1976

The only climber to be awarded AARS in the past 20 years. The intensely
fragrant, bright pink flowers are produced over a long season and are as
beautiful as the best hybrid tea.

Flower and Fragrance
Perfectly formed, coral-pink buds open into high-centered pink blossoms with a
silvery sheen. Double, 4 to 5 inches, with 30 to 35 petals. Borne in clusters. Strong
spicy fragrance.

Form and Foliage
Strong-growing, upright plant of medium height. Fully covered with medium
green leaves. Lacks vigor and hardiness in cold climates.

Blaze   ARS 7.4 Introduced 1932

Probably the most popular and widely planted climbing rose. Valued for its
continuous bloom, bright red flowers and problem-free growth wherever it is
planted. Unequaled as a landscape plant on a fence, pillar or trellis. Sometimes
called 'Improved Paul's Scarlet'.

Flower and Fragrance
Scarlet-red buds open into deep red, cup-shaped blooms. Double, 2 to 3 inches,
with 20 to 25 petals. Borne in large clusters. Slight fragrance.

Form and Foliage
Vigorous and upright but slightly smaller than other climbers. Dark green,
semiglossy foliage. Hardy and disease resistant.

Don Juan   ARS 8.2 Introduced 1958

A beautiful, long-stemmed, red-flowering climber best adapted to hot-summer,
mild-winter climates. Ideal for trellis, small fence or pillar.

Flower and Fragrance
Pointed buds open into nicely shaped, velvety red blossoms. Double, 4 to 5
inches, with 30 to 35 petals. Borne singly and in clusters. Highly fragrant.

Form and Foliage
Medium-tall, vigorous and upright plant. Shiny, dark green leaves. Disease
resistant but not reliably cold hardy.

Dortmund

ARS 9.1 Introduced 1955

A versatile and spectacular, single-flowering climber. Large clusters of bright red flowers with white centers. Can also be used as a mounding shrub or sprawling ground cover. Good repeat bloom.

Flower and Fragrance

Slender pointed buds open into flat, bright red blossoms with white centers. Single, 3 to 3-1/2 inches, with 5 to 7 petals. Borne in large clusters. Moderate fragrance.

Form and Foliage

Vigorous, medium-tall plant with glossy, dark green leaves. Disease resistant and cold hardy.

Dublin Bay

ARS 8.5 Introduced 1975

A profuse-blooming, large-flowering climber with fragrant red flowers. Excellent repeat bloom. Easily trained.

Flower and Fragrance

Ovoid buds open into cup-shaped, bright red blossoms. Double, 4-1/2 inches, with 25 petals. Borne in clusters. Moderate fragrance.

Form and Foliage

Vigorous and upright, medium to tall plant with dark green, leathery leaves. Disease resistant and cold hardy.

Golden Showers

ARS 7.1 Introduced 1956, AARS 1957

One of only four climbers to win AARS, and deserving of the honor. Covers itself with sunny yellow flowers that produce an alluring, licorice scent. Continuous bloom on an easy-to-manage plant, ideal for fence or trellis.

Flower and Fragrance

Lemon-yellow buds open into clear yellow, cup-shaped blossoms. Double, 3 to 4 inches, with 25 to 30 petals. Borne in clusters. Moderate fragrance.

Form and Foliage

Short, compact plant, with strong stems and shiny, dark green leaves. Disease resistant and hardy.

Handel

ARS 8.2 Introduced 1965

A lovely, creamy white rose with a light pink edge. Consistent bloom on a strong-growing plant. Easily trained on fence, trellis or post.

Flower and Fragrance

Shapely, light pink buds open into cream white blossoms with pink edges. Double, 3 to 4 inches, with 20 to 25 petals. Borne singly and in small clusters. Slight fragrance.

Form and Foliage

Tall and vigorous growth. Shiny, medium green leaves. Disease resistant and cold hardy.

■ ■ ■

Classic Climbers

A traditional way to use climbing roses in the landscape is to plant red-flowering varieties such as 'Blaze' or 'Altissimo' on a white picket fence or rail fence. The contrast of the deep red flowers and dark green leaves against the white fence creates a inviting, country-Victorian look.

■ ■ ■

Right: 'America' has intensely fragrant, bright pink flowers that bloom generously over a long period. Plant is medium sized, disease resistant and cold hardy.

Below: 'Blaze' (also known as 'Improved Paul's Scarlet') is probably the most popular and widely planted climber. Plant is vigorous and upright, attaining a slightly smaller mature size compared to most other climbers.

Below right: 'Dortmund' (also shown on page 136) is a versatile climber that can be used as a mounding shrub or sprawling ground cover.

Left: 'Dublin Bay' is an easy-to-train climber with excellent repeat bloom. Flowers are large, up to 4-1/2 inches across, and have a strong fragrance.

Below left: 'Handel' also adapts easily to training. Plants are vigorous, tall growing and disease resistant.

Below: 'Don Juan' is not as cold hardy as other climbers, so it is best grown in mild-winter regions. The large, 4-1/2-inch flowers are quite fragrant.

Support for Climbers

Climbing roses don't twine, cling with tendrils or physically attach themselves to supports as many common vines do, so they require some assistance to "climb." Tie canes to supports with cotton twine or garden ties, or weave the canes through fences or around posts. On solid walls, use lattice supports or stretch wires between eye-bolts or screws. Many nurseries or hardware stores also carry wall attachments or "vine hangers" designed to adhere to walls.

■ ■ ■

High Noon
ARS 7.2 Introduced 1948, AARS 1948

A free-flowering, climbing hybrid tea with bright yellow flowers touched with red. One of only four climbing roses to have been designated AARS.

Flower and Fragrance
Deep yellow buds swirl open into bright yellow blossoms with red on the outsides of petals. Double, 3 to 4 inches, with 25 to 30 petals. Borne singly. Moderately spicy fragrance.

Form and Foliage
Vigorous, small to medium-sized climber with leathery, bright green leaves. Disease resistant and cold hardy.

Joseph's Coat
ARS 7.6 Introduced 1964

Few roses are as colorful as this large-flowering climber. The word "kaleidoscopic" is often used to describe the flowers, which continuously change colors from golden yellow to orange to red. A small plant, ideal for an everblooming fence cover.

Flower and Fragrance
Shapely red buds open into multicolored blooms of yellow, orange and red. Double, 3 to 4 inches, with 25 to 30 petals. Borne in clusters. Slight fragrance.

Form and Foliage
Vigorous, small to medium-sized plant with glossy green leaves. Tends to mildew and is not reliably hardy.

Lace Cascade
ARS ___ Introduced 1992

A recent introduction that quickly gained notoriety and won many prestigious awards. A vigorous, clean-foliaged climber with beautiful white blooms. Can be grown on fence or trellis or as an arching shrub. Resists mildew.

Flower and Fragrance
Creamy white buds open into full, white blossoms borne in clusters. Double, 3-1/2 to 4 inches, with 25 to 40 petals. Pleasing fragrance.

Form and Foliage
Tall (to 7 feet), vigorous plant with attractive, dark green leaves.

New Dawn
ARS 7.9 Introduced 1930

A vigorous pink rose that has the distinction of being the first plant ever patented. A free-blooming sport of 'Dr. W. Van Fleet'. Useful in climbing over a trellis or sprawling on a bank. Good cut flower.

Flower and Fragrance
Small, light pink buds open into blush pink, cup-shaped blossoms with yellow stamens. Double, 3 to 3-1/2 inches, with 20 to 25 petals. Borne in small clusters. Moderate fragrance.

Form and Foliage
A vigorous plant that can easily grow more than 15 feet high. Shiny, dark green leaves. Disease resistant and cold hardy.

Piñata
ARS 7.0 Introduced 1978

A bright, multicolored climber that is similar to 'Joseph's Coat'. Well behaved, perfect for a low fence or small trellis. Can be a shy bloomer. See photo page 29.

Flower and Fragrance
Light yellow and red, egg-shaped buds open into yellow blossoms edged with orange-red. Double, 2-1/2 to 3 inches, with 25 to 30 petals. Borne in large clusters. Slight fragrance.

Form and Foliage
Low growing and easily maintained at a height of 6 to 8 feet. Dense, glossy, deep green leaves. Disease resistant and cold hardy.

Royal Gold
ARS 7.5 Introduced 1957

A sunny yellow rose with a delightful, fruity fragrance. Flowers maintain bright color even in heat. An easy-to-train plant, perfect for fence or small trellis. Good cut flower.

Flower and Fragrance
Shapely buds open into hybrid tea-like, golden yellow blossoms. Double, 3 to 4 inches, with 30 to 40 petals. Borne singly and in clusters. Moderately fruity fragrance.

Form and Foliage
Well-behaved, small to medium-sized plant easily maintained at 6 to 8 feet. Glossy, deep green foliage. Few thorns. Disease resistant and cold hardy.

Tempo
ARS 7.5 Introduced 1975

Easily trained, well behaved and everblooming describe this deep red flowering climber. One of the easiest and best landscape roses for fence, trellis and arbor.

Flower and Fragrance
Dark red buds swirl open into shapely bright blossoms. Double, 3-1/2 to 4 inches, with 35 to 45 petals. Borne in clusters. Slight fragrance.

Form and Foliage
Strong-growing, medium-sized plant with shiny, deep green foliage. Disease resistant and cold hardy. Best performance in the West.

White Dawn
ARS 7.0 Introduced 1949

Large clusters of ruffled white flowers resembling gardenias grace this popular, large-flowering climber. Plant is everblooming and is a wonderful selection to brighten a fence or trellis.

Flower and Fragrance
Shapely white buds open into clean white blossoms with ruffled petals. Double, 2 to 3 inches, with 30 to 35 petals. Borne in clusters. Slight fragrance.

Form and Foliae
Vigorous, medium-sized plant with shiny green leaves. Disease resistant.

PLANTING AND CARE

Roses are plants that like to grow. After they're established, they require about the same amount of care as other landscape plants. If you're new to growing roses, this may come as a surprise. Perhaps it is the delicate appearance of their flowers that makes people believe the plants are fragile and require special care. Or maybe it's the fact that since roses bloom almost continuously they need more frequent attention. Beginning rose growers may be intimidated by the often-meticulous gardening practices of *rosarians*, experts in growing roses, who work hard to produce perfect flowers and win accolades at rose shows. The newcomer might well conclude: "If that's what the experts do, then that's what I'll do."

The fact is, how you grow roses is a matter of personal preference. If you don't spray, fertilize and prune plants regularly, you won't have as many flowers, but you'll still have blooms. The look of your rose garden will match your interest level. Most roses are vigorous-growing, hardy plants that can survive and bloom even when neglected. This is especially true today, with more attention paid to developing disease-resistant varieties.

Like most landscape plants, roses require attention to the basics. They should be planted properly and given regular water and fertilizer. In cold climates, roses need protection from severe winter weather. For the natural rose gardener, simple cultural practices like watering and fertilizing take on special significance. Stressed plants seem to send out an invitation to pests and diseases. Keeping any plant healthy and growing vigorously is one of the surest ways to prevent problems so that chemical controls are not necessary.

To put on a decent show of high-quality blooms, the goal of most gardeners, rose plants require *attention* but not necessarily a lot of *time*. It's mostly a matter of checking plants regularly, perhaps a few times each week. This is particularly important if you wish to eliminate (or greatly reduce) use of chemical sprays. Inspecting plants frequently exposes problems in the beginning stages, when they are easier to correct with natural controls. This is true whether it's an infestation of insects or diseases or the first signs of stress due to lack of water.

The following pages present step-by-step information and illustrations describing how to plant, water, fertilize and prune roses, plus guidelines on identifying and controlling common pests and diseases. Selecting regionally adapted, disease-resistant varieties and planting them in the right location will prevent many problems. For a list of rose varieties adapted to specific climate regions, see pages 28 to 30. For details about individual roses and the basic rose forms, refer to "Gallery of Roses," pages 36 to 143.

Planting roses in well-prepared soil where plants will receive at least six hours of sun a day will help get your plants off to a good start.

Planting Bareroot Roses

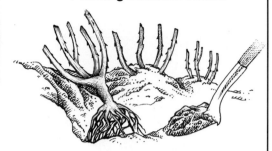

Heel-in roses that must be stored temporarily before planting. Place on an angle in a shallow trench and cover roots with moist organic matter or soil.

Dig a hole that is about as deep as the depth of the root system. Form a small cone of soil in the bottom of the hole.

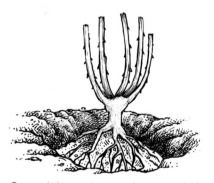

Spread the roots over the mound of soil, making sure the rose is planted an inch or two higher than it was at the nursery. Look for the dark soil line on the trunk.

Fill in soil around the roots. Form soil basin and water well. To prevent canes from drying, cover one-third of the height with soil or organic matter. Remove this soil covering when growth begins.

Getting Started

Roses can be purchased in two ways—either bareroot or in containers. *Bareroot* plants, as their name suggests, are sold and shipped without soil around their roots. They are available when plants are dormant—during the cold winter months, usually beginning in early December. Mail-order nurseries generally ship to their customers during this period. The length of the bareroot season varies depending on where you live. In cold-winter climates the season may extend into the early months of spring. In milder climates, such as the deep South or the Southwest, warmer weather as early as February may cause bareroot roses to start growing. At that point most nurseries will plant their bareroot roses in containers and sell them at a slightly higher cost.

Bareroot Roses

During winter, plants are dug in commercial growing fields, and often packed with moist material such as a loose mulch or ground wood product around their roots and enclosed in plastic. This is less expensive and less labor intensive than potting and caring for plants in containers, so bareroot roses are usually cheaper to purchase. These bareroot roses are then distributed through local nurseries, garden centers and mail-order sources. Plants not individually packaged are usually shipped in bulk to nurseries and placed in large beds of moist organic matter. Many mail-order nurseries ship plants in boxes packed with moist organic material.

Bareroot roses are graded by standards set by the American Association of Nurserymen. The grades—*No. 1, No. 1-1/2* and *No. 2*—are based on the number and size of canes. No. 1's are the highest-quality plants. Most experienced rose growers believe that the additional expense of No. 1-grade rose plants is money well spent. If you purchase a lesser-grade rose plant, you're taking a chance that it will be weak, requiring much longer to reach full vigor and optimum bloom.

If you purchase bareroot roses, take special care that plants do not dry out. As soon as you bring your roses home from the retail outlet or receive them in the mail, remove the outside packaging material and check to see if the packing around the roots is moist. If dry, soak the roots in a bucket of water for no longer than 12 hours. If the packing is moist, store plants in a cool, dark location until planting time.

It's best to plant bareroot roses as soon as possible after purchasing. If possible, prepare planting sites (including any necessary soil preparation) right after you place your order. Roses can then go into the ground right after you purchase them or receive them in the mail. However, if poor weather or lack of time prevents this, keep the moistened packing material around the roots and store plants in a cool place (35F to 40F). Check the packing material every few days to be sure it remains moist. *Do not allow roots to dry out at any time.* Bareroot roses can generally be stored this way for one to two weeks. The warmer the conditions, the shorter the allowable storage time.

If you bought several bareroot roses and are unable to plant within a week or two, protect them by *heeling-in*. Dig a trench about one foot deep in a cool, shady area. Lay plants in the trench at a 45-degree angle, then cover roots and the lower third of the branches with moist soil or mulch. Keep roots moist until planting time. An alternative to heeling-in is to pot up roses in containers until you can plant them.

This works especially well if more than a few weeks will pass until plants go into the ground.

Before planting bareroot roses, soak roots in muddy water for several hours. Use pruning shears to remove all broken or damaged roots. Make all cuts sharp and clean.

Planting Roses from Containers

After the weather begins to warm in spring, the buds of bareroot roses will begin to swell. This is the time most retail nurseries plant remaining bareroot rose stock in containers and sell them as potted plants. Container roses are usually more expensive than bareroot plants, but they provide gardeners with an extended planting period. Note: If you buy container roses early in the season and they are recent bareroot transplants, make sure plants have had sufficient time to develop root systems. Plants may have difficulty surviving if planted too soon after going from bareroot to container plant.

Container-planted roses require careful attention to watering after planting, but they can be planted practically any time.

If you are planting container-grown roses that are actively growing, keep your pre-plant pruning to a minimum. Latest research shows that unless the rootball is damaged, it's best to leave as much foliage as possible. This way the leaves can manufacture the food necessary for a quick establishment.

Selecting Planting Sites

Roses grow best when planted in an area that receives 6 to 8 hours of direct sun. They will accept less sunlight, but plants may be rangier, have sparser foliage and produce fewer flowers. Because reduced sunlight does not allow them to grow to their potential, most roses planted in shade become more susceptible to diseases.

When considering planting sites, it is helpful to recognize the *microclimates* around your house. A microclimate is a small climate zone that differs from the general surrounding climate. Exposure to sun and wind, topography and air drainage, as well as proximity to large objects such as buildings (your house) and trees, create areas that are warmer, cooler or windier. This is particularly true if you live in an area that has climatic extremes. If the hot desert Southwest, for example, planting on the east side of your home protects roses from the hottest afternoon sun. At the same time, plants receive plenty of the less intense morning and midday sunshine. These slightly milder conditions can make all the difference with varieties of roses that weaken in high heat. Less heat also reduces the plant's water needs.

In cool, cloudy climates, such as in the Pacific Northwest, the goal may be to maximize the heat around a particular rose. This can be accomplished by planting near a warm south- or west-facing wall. The heat radiated from the wall may be just enough to fully open that multipetaled red rose that never quite reached peak bloom. It could also help curtail diseases that flourish in cool, wet conditions.

As mentioned, trees affect microclimates by creating cooling shade. But they can also cause serious problems. It's best to avoid planting roses close to large trees with greedy roots. They literally suck the water and nutrients away from your roses, making it difficult to keep plants healthy.

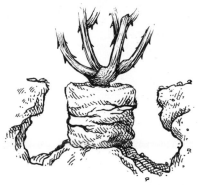

Dig a hole slightly shallower than the depth of the rootball. Remove the rootball from the container and gently loosen circling roots.

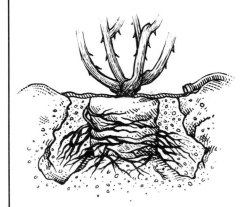

Fill in the hole with soil. Build a soil basin and water thoroughly.

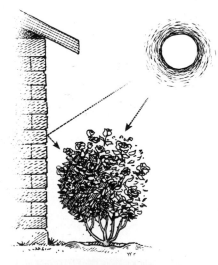

In cool climates, planting roses against south-facing walls takes advantage of additional heat to improve the flowering of some varieties. Also see page 12.

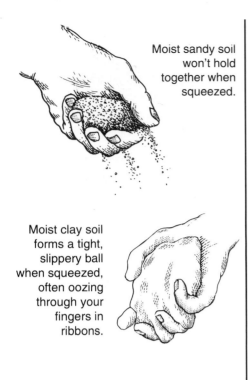

Moist sandy soil won't hold together when squeezed.

Moist clay soil forms a tight, slippery ball when squeezed, often oozing through your fingers in ribbons.

Moist loam soil forms a loose ball when squeezed. It falls apart easily when touched.

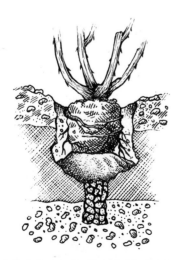

If soil drainage is slow due to hardpan, dig a "chimney" to reach the well-draining soil below.

Soils

Roses will grow in most soils, from light sandy soils to heavy clay. Rose plants do demand one thing—*good drainage.* In poorly draining soils, the roots suffocate from lack of oxygen and become susceptible to soil-borne diseases. To be certain your soil drains properly, test for drainage before you plant. Dig the planting hole according to the instructions on page 147, then fill the hole with water. After the water has drained completely, fill it again. The water should drain within 24 hours. If it does not, the best solution is to admit defeat and plant in a different location where drainage is sufficient. If you have no choice but to plant in a particular site, you can try creating a *drainage chimney.* Dig a narrow channel (the chimney) through the impeding layer of soil. This allows excess water to drain away from the root area. See the illustration below left. Other options include building a raised bed or mounded berm of well-draining soil; or plant roses in large containers, such as half whiskey barrels.

Regional Guide to Planting, Pruning & Fertilizing				
	Plant Bareroot	Plant Containers	Fertilize	Dormant Prune**
California	Dec-Jan	Year-round*	Mar-Oct	Jan-Feb
Pacific Northwest	Jan-Feb	Year-round*	Mar-Aug	Jan-Feb
Deep South	Dec-Jan	Year-round*	Feb-Nov^	Jan
Mid-South	Jan-Feb	Year-round*	Mar-Oct	Feb-Mar
Midwest & Northeast	Mar-Apr#	Mar-Dec	Mar-Aug	Mar-Apr
Desert	Dec-Jan	Year-round*	Mar-Nov	Jan-Feb

  * *Cool months preferred*
 ** *Can be done whenever plants are dormant*
 ^ *Some fertilize year-round but lighter doses during cool months*
 # *Can plant earlier if soil can be worked*

Soil pH

Local experts are often the best source of advice on how to correct soil problems in your area. In the western United States, soils are often *alkaline.* This means the soil has a pH above 7.0. Roses grow best in soil with a pH between 6.5 and 7.0. Many gardeners in the Southwest prefer to add soil sulfur and gypsum and use acidifying fertilizers to make soils less alkaline. They also use products containing iron to prevent iron chlorosis (yellowing of the foliage), another malady common in alkaline soils.

In the Pacific Northwest and eastern United States, soils are *acidic,* meaning they have a pH below 7.0. In these areas, acid soils can be neutralized by adding dolomitic lime.

If you suspect that the pH of your soil is too high or too low for roses, you can test it. Do-it-yourself kits can be purchased in local nurseries or through mail-order outlets, or you can send a soil sample to a soil lab for a more sophisticated test. Although more expensive, a professional test can also measure your soil's fertility and texture. Your county cooperative extension service can recommend soil labs in your area.

Improving Soils

Horticulturists are divided on the issue of whether to add organic matter to the soil before planting trees and shrubs. Some believe it's best to get plant roots established in native soil as soon as possible. Adding organic matter creates a *transition* between the amended soil and native soil that may prevent roots from spreading as wide as possible. Most horticulturists believe that adding organic matter to the soil improves plant growth. Amendments can help sandy soils retain water and nutrients in the root zone and increases aeration in clay or compacted soils.

The fact is, many gardeners must deal with difficult soils. Soil problems can be particularly serious around new home developments, where the original topsoil has been removed during construction. It makes sense that adding organic matter such as compost, leaf mold, peat moss, ground bark or decomposed animal manures to problem soils would improve, not hinder a plant's ability to grow.

If your soil is dense, heavy clay or very sandy, add some organic matter to the backfill (soil that was dug to make the planting hole) at planting time. The amendment should make up about one-third of the soil that goes into the planting hole. Mix well. If you're preparing for a mass planting over a large area, cover the soil with 3 to 4 inches of organic matter. Work it to a depth of 6 to 8 inches with a shovel or rototiller. Be aware, however, that if your soil has poor drainage, adding organic matter will not solve the problem. The impervious layer that impedes drainage will continue to hold water in the root zone. This layer must be removed or broken through so water can move down and away from the root zone.

Watering

Roses need water on a regular basis to keep them growing actively and blooming continuously. *How much* and *how often* vary according to many factors, including the season, soil type and exposure to the sun. Plants growing in light, fast-draining sandy soil need more frequent irrigation than those growing in heavier clay soil. In hot or windy weather, plants *transpire* at a more rapid rate, so they require more water than in cool, cloudy weather.

Newly planted roses, like all plants, need water much more frequently than established plants. In hot-summer regions, it could be as often as every day. Established plants accept less frequent irrigation; once each week is usually enough.

The best watering schedule is one you develop on your own through experience and observation. Pay careful attention to seasonal and day-to-day variables mentioned above, including temperature, rainfall and wind. Learn to recognize early signs of water need, such as leaves becoming lackluster in color, taking on a grayish green cast. If new growth begins to droop and wilt, it's a sure sign of a serious lack of moisture and plants should be watered immediately.

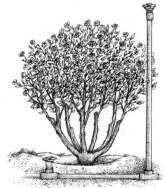

Overhead or ground-level watering? Each has advantages and disadvantages. Overhead watering cleanses the foliage, but evaporation is high and it can encourage diseases. A ground-level irrigation system waters efficiently, but it can be difficult to cultivate around plants.

Drip irrigation applies water at a slow, even rate, preventing runoff. Because it wets a smaller area, weed growth is reduced.

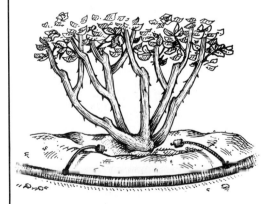

Drip emitters apply water at different rates, usually expressed in *gallons per hour*, which determine the duration that roses receive water. One to two emitters per plant is usually enough.

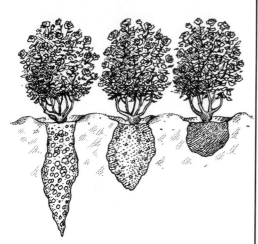

Soil type greatly affects depth of water penetration. By comparison, from left: sandy soil, loam soil, clay soil.

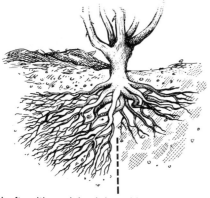

Left: with mulch, right: without. By cooling soil, conserving moisture, and reducing weeds, a layer of mulch encourages healthier root growth near the soil surface.

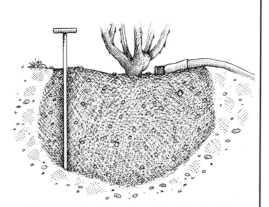

Roses prefer deep watering. To check how deep water has reached, push a steel rod into the soil after irrigation. The rod will penetrate the same depth as the water.

Ways to Apply Water

If you have only two or three plants, it may be easiest to build soil basins around each one and soak the soil with water from a hand-held hose. As the number of roses in your landscape increases, this method becomes too time-consuming and inefficient. Consider a permanent, automated irrigation system. Automated irrigation systems not only save time, they allow you to regulate how much water each plant receives and when. You can also determine how water is applied, whether through sprinklers or drip-irrigation emitters.

The first step in installing an irrigation system is making a scale drawing of your yard or garden. Take this to an irrigation supply store where a trained designer can help you create a system to meet the needs of your plants.

Where you live can influence the system's design. For example, in hot, dry climates, some rose growers prefer to water with overhead sprinklers. They believe frequent, early morning "rains" cleanse the foliage and help curtail certain insects and diseases. In regions where summer rains are common, growers tend to favor ground-level micro-sprinklers or bubblers so that foliage remains dry. This also helps reduce infestations of water-spread diseases. In the arid West, water conservation is a part of everyday life and a drip-irrigation system is practically a necessity. Drip systems apply water slowly and frequently to a small, confined area around the plant's roots. They eliminate wasteful runoff and reduce weeds by wetting the soil only around the root area. When installed and used properly, drip irrigation can reduce outdoor water use up to 70 percent.

For help in determining the irrigation system right for your garden situation, contact the nearest chapter of the American Rose Society.

Watering Tips

How much water to apply to plants each session is as important as *how often* to water. As a guide, wet the soil to a depth of about 18 inches. In sandy soils, this should require about 1 inch of water. In clay soils, it may take three times as much. Check water penetration by probing the soil with a long, narrow rod or screwdriver. The probe moves easily through wet soil and halts when it hits dry soil.

The best time of day to water roses is early morning. Winds are usually less prevalent at this time, and the lower temperatures reduce water loss through evaporation. Most important, the foliage dries out during the day (unlike with evening applications), avoiding the moist conditions that encourage serious rose diseases such as downy mildew and black spot.

Mulching

A mulch is a layer of material, usually organic, applied around plants to aid their growth. Common mulches include compost, ground bark, straw, pine needles and even shredded newspapers. A 3- to 4-inch layer of mulch around the root area of your roses will cool the soil and conserve soil moisture by reducing evaporation. In addition, as organic mulches decompose, they help improve the soil.

A mulch also helps smother weeds, which compete for water and nutrients. Weeds that do grow in a mulch are much easier to remove. This is particularly important with roses, because their surface roots can be easily damaged when cultivating around the root area. Applying a mulch reduces the need to cultivate.

Fertilizing Roses

When fertilizing newly planted roses, *do not* place fertilizer in the planting hole, where it can burn the roots. Rather, plant the rose as shown in the illustrations on pages 146 and 147, sprinkle fertilizer on the soil surface over the root area, and water well.

Feed established roses every four to six weeks to keep plants healthy and blooming continuously. Make the first application just as the buds begin to swell in spring. Continue feeding until August in cold-winter climates, up to October in mild-winter regions. See chart on page 148.

If you're new to growing roses, it is easiest to purchase a complete, granular rose fertilizer that contains the basic elements: *nitrogen, phosphorus* and *potassium*. Some formulations also include minor nutrients such as iron. The ratios of the essential nutrients are listed as percentages on the product, always in the same order. For example, a 10-5-10 contains 10 percent nitrogen, 5 percent phosphorus and 10 percent potassium.

Apply commercial rose fertilizers according to the label instructions. Don't increase the recommended amount, thinking it will cause your roses to grow even better—it will probably do more harm than good. Make sure plants are well watered before applying fertilizers. This is particularly important with recently planted roses.

Natural Organic Fertilizers

Experienced rose growers know that composted animal manures and fish emulsion are natural sources of nitrogen and other nutrients. They are less expensive than commercially available products and can be effective "rose food." In addition, animal manures decompose to improve the soil. One drawback to their use is that the exact amounts of nutrients to be applied are not as precise. As a guide, fish emulsion is usually 5 percent nitrogen; most composted manures range from 2 percent to 4 percent nitrogen. Use only aged, well-rotted manures to fertilize roses. Fresh, uncomposted manures contain toxic salts that can burn roots and leaves, even kill plants.

In some instances, the nutrients in animal manures may not be immediately "available" to plants. For example, organic fertilizers such as composted manures and blood meal must be broken down by soil organisms before the plant can absorb the nutrients. How quickly materials are processed depends on the soil temperature; the warmer the soil the sooner the nutrients can be absorbed by plants. What this means is that in cool weather, organic fertilizers may not provide enough nitrogen for plants; in hot-summer regions they may provide too much, burning plants. Only with experience in your own garden will you be able to determine *"how much and how often."*

Pruning

Why prune roses? Pruning helps keep rose plants shapely, healthy and free-blooming. How much plants are pruned depends on the type of rose and time of year, as well as its use in the landscape. In general, hybrid teas and grandifloras are pruned the most severely. *Hard pruning,* cutting back severely to a few canes, encourages fewer but larger flowers. Climbing roses are pruned to keep them within bounds and attached to their supports. *Light pruning* produces numerous but smaller flowers.

Fertilizer labels provide necessary information about nutrient content and the composition of the product by weight. Nutrients are always listed in this order: *nitrogen, phosphorus, potassium.*

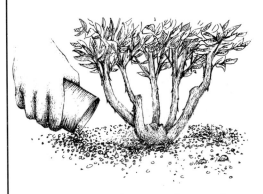

Apply granular fertilizers evenly around the base of the plant. Water thoroughly.

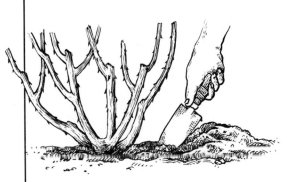

Dig compost or composted animal manures into the root zone around roses, being careful not to damage the shallow roots. Water well.

An unpruned hybrid tea will have many canes. As a guide, reduce the overall size by one-third to one-half.

For good flower production, prune hybrid teas back to 3 to 6 strong canes. Canes should be well spaced, leaving the center of the plant open.

When making pruning cuts, cut about 1/4 inch above an *outward-facing* eye. This helps develop an open, spreading plant.

Shrub roses and species roses are pruned least. Roses used in mass plantings in the landscape can often be sheared like a hedge.

Experienced rose growers are seldom out among their plants without their pruning shears, often in sheaths attached to their belts. As they move among their plants, inspecting them, they continually remove spent flowers to encourage new blooms. This is called *deadheading*. They also trim off suckers or pinch off wayward branches. In this sense, light pruning is performed almost 12 months a year.

The primary time to prune roses is in early spring, just as the buds begin to swell. This is the time to access the health of each plant, selecting the strongest branches for future flowers and removing branches that are weak or withered.

To prune your roses, arm yourself with a thick pair of gloves and sharp, *scissor-type* pruning shears that have a *curved* blade. These kinds of shears are recommended because they make the cleanest cuts. If you are working on older plants, you'll also need a pruning saw and long-handled loppers to remove large canes and dead wood.

Pruning Hybrid Teas

Remove dead or damaged wood. Cut back dead or broken branches flush with the base of the plant. Healthy canes are green; dead canes are brown and shriveled.

Remove suckers. *Suckers* are vigorous canes that originate from the rootstock *below* the bud union. They sap the plant's energy that should go toward making leaves and flowers. Suckers have a different appearance, with smaller leaves compared to those on desirable canes. Remove suckers whenever you notice them. Pull the soil away from the base of the plant and use a sharp knife to remove suckers at their origin.

Select flower-producing canes. Choose the healthiest canes. These will produce flowers the coming season. Keep those that are spaced evenly around the plant so it will develop a strong structure. Remove all spindly growth and canes that crisscross, keeping the center of the plant open. Reduce the overall height by one-third to one-half. Make each cut about 1/4 inch above an *eye* that faces away from the center of the plant. Eyes are the dormant buds that will grow into flowering shoots. See the illustration at below left. After pruning, remove and destroy all old leaves remaining on plant to reduce overwintering of diseases.

The interior of a healthy cane will be whitish in color. If it is brown the cane has probably suffered some damage. Cut it back farther until the wood looks healthy or remove it entirely.

Pruning Other Rose Forms

Grandifloras are pruned using the same steps as hybrid teas. The major exception is that grandifloras can usually support more flowering canes.

To prune miniatures, follow the same principles as with hybrid teas. Remove all dead wood. Reduce the height to two-thirds to three-quarters of the original plant size.

Floribundas usually have more twiggy growth than hybrid teas, especially near the center of the plant. Prune so there are more small, evenly spaced canes. Remove all dead wood and crossing canes.

When pruning a tree rose, approach the job as if the top of the plant were growing at ground level. From a design standpoint, the goal is to develop flowering canes so flowers will be at eye level. Maintain tree roses so they have a balanced, rounded head. Remove suckers along the trunk to maintain the tree form.

Train large-flowering climbers and climbing sports so they produce main structural canes that are in proportion to the size and shape of the supports. For example, climbers growing along a sturdy fence should be trained to produce several permanent main canes. Leave short flowering canes along the length of the main canes if you want the main cane to continue increasing in length. The goal is to create a balanced structure with evenly spaced, horizontally trained main canes. If necessary, replace diseased or damaged main canes with vigorous new shoots rising from the base of the plant. Be sure these new shoots originate *above* the bud union. Note that some climbers bloom only on second-year growth. If you prune them too hard, flower production will be greatly reduced. See the illustration at right.

Many ramblers bloom only in spring and should be pruned after they cease flowering. Depending on the function of the plants in the landscape, flowering canes can be cut back to the ground to encourage new growth, which will bloom the following spring. If ramblers are used in the landscape, lightly trim back plants to encourage new growth all over the plant.

Pruning Shrub Roses and Old Garden Roses

Shrub roses and old garden roses represent such a varied group of plants it is difficult to provide definitive rules for pruning. It is best to treat them like other shrublike plants in the landscape and adjust your pruning according to the situation, whether it's formal, informal or natural. In general, thin out old or diseased canes so plants remain healthy and full-foliaged. Feel free to lightly shear plants after bloom (if you don't want hips, rose fruit, to develop) and cut back wayward branches. During the winter dormant season, reduce the size of plants only if necessary to keep plants within bounds of available space.

Some of the more vigorous shrubs and old garden roses will produce more blooms if long canes are arched or pegged to the ground. This works particularly well with many of the David Austin and Meidiland roses. See page 47.

If you have floribundas, miniatures or other landscape roses in a mass planting, use pruning shears to cut back about half of each plant. Create a mound shape so flowers will bloom all over the plant.

Vigorous old garden roses such as lady Banks rose, sprawling shrubs like selections of the Meidiland roses and even many climbers can be left unpruned to create wildlife habitats, thorny barriers, hedges or natural background plantings. Flowers will probably be smaller and the plants may not repeat bloom as often, but they will serve as attractive and useful landscape plants.

Summer Pruning and Grooming

Most rose forms require a certain amount of care during the summer months when plants are actively growing. Many require *deadheading*, as shown in the drawing above right. Another summer chore is *disbudding*, also shown at right. This is the removal of small, side flowerbuds to increase the size of the main bud. (But be aware it does

Train climbers by tying permanent structural canes to support. Along their length, cut back flowering canes to 2 to 3 buds.

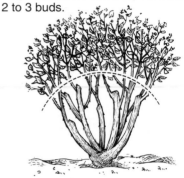

Floribundas, miniatures and many shrub roses can be easily pruned with shears. Cut back about half the plant, creating a mound-shaped form.

Deadheading, removing spent flowers, encourages the rose plant to produce more blooms.

Disbudding is the removal of small side flower buds. It channels energy into the main flower, resulting in a larger flower.

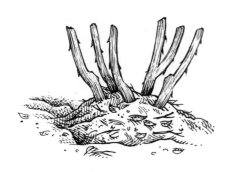

Mounding soil or mulch over the base of the plant is one of the simplest forms of winter protection.

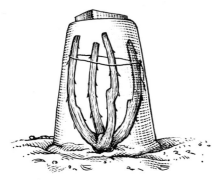

Wrap roses in a wire cylinder and fill with straw or other organic matter to provide a greater degree of winter protection.

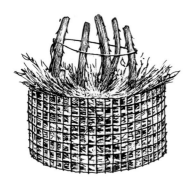

A manufactured styrofoam protection cap (ideally filled with organic matter) topped with a brick is effective winter protection.

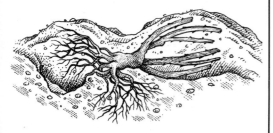

In severe winter areas, dig up or cut one side of the root system, tip the plant on its side, and cover with soil or organic matter.

decrease overall bloom.) During the growing season it is also much easier to distinguish *suckers* from the desirable *basal breaks*, vigorous new shoots that rise from above the bud union and look the same as the rest of the plant. Suckers, as described on page 152, have a "different" look. Basal breaks are good candidates to become flowering canes the next spring and should be left to grow. If they become too tall, cut back to 1-1/2 to 2 feet high.

In hot-summer climates, it is best to prune lightly during summer. Retaining as much foliage on the plant as possible helps avoid sunburn damage to the canes.

Winter Protection

Most roses accept cold temperatures down to 15F to 20F. If your average low temperature in winter falls below this, or if you are growing varieties that are less cold hardy, the winter protection methods shown on these pages will help prevent your roses from being damaged or killed by the cold. Whichever method you use, don't take protection measures too early; it could do more harm than good. Plants need about two weeks of below-freezing temperatures to become *hardened-off*—gradually adapted to the cold weather. If plants are protected before their tissues are allowed to reach maximum hardiness, they are actually more susceptible to winter damage. Wait until cold temperatures have settled in for a couple of weeks before protecting plants.

Prepare roses for cooler temperatures by watering them well in fall so adequate soil moisture will be available during winter. Do not fertilize after late summer or early fall. Additional nutrients at this time will encourage new, tender growth that is much more susceptible to cold damage. Wait to fertilize the following spring.

About the easiest way to protect roses is to cover the base of the plant with about 12 inches of soil or mulch.. Do this in fall. After the weather has been cold for a couple of weeks, wrap or cover the rest of the plant with an insulating mulch; straw or pine boughs work well. You can also wrap roses in man-made insulating materials such as foam rubber, filling in around the plant with straw or mulch.

Climbing roses require a slightly different approach. Wrap plants on their supports, or untie the canes, lay them on the ground and cover with soil or mulch. Tree roses can be wrapped with insulating material. In extreme conditions, carefully dig up the roots on one side of the plant so it can be laid on the ground and cover with soil or mulch. See illustration below left.

Controlling Pests and Diseases

Like most plants, roses are occasionally bothered by insects and diseases. In the past, it was common to reach for a chemical spray at the first sign of trouble. Many exhibitors who display their flowers in rose shows spray on a regular basis to prevent pests and diseases. This *preventive* spray program calls for applying various fungicides and insecticides every 7 to 10 days during the growing season. However, for most rose gardeners, this is impractical and unnecessary.

Today's gardener has a wide range of choices when it comes to selecting methods of pest and disease control. This applies to all kinds of gardening, whether it's vegetables, landscape plants or roses. It becomes a matter of what kind of results you are comfortable with and how "natural" you want your controls to be. Sooner or later, you'll probably have to choose between using sprays to combat a serious infestation or allowing the pest or disease to seriously damage or kill your plants. Before you take steps to control the offender, be certain you've correctly identified the problem. If necessary, take samples of the afflicted plant parts to your rose society, nursery or county extension agent to get positive identification.

After you've selected the product for control, *follow the instructions on the label exactly.* You are risking *your* health, and the health of your plants, if you don't. Do not spray on windy days. Spraying when plants are in need of moisture may cause leaves to burn. Wear rubber gloves when handling concentrates, and never store pesticides in unmarked containers. Clean sprayers away from plants after each use.

A Prevention Program

The best method of controlling pests and diseases is preventing them from getting established in your garden. Making a few basic practices part of your gardening routine will go a long way in preventing most pest and disease problems on your roses as well as in the rest of your garden. This will allow you to eliminate or greatly reduce spraying and other chemical means of pest and disease control.

Grow disease-resistant rose varieties. Descriptions in the "Gallery of Roses" include information on relative disease resistance. Also see the list of disease-resistant roses on page 31.

Keep plants healthy. Plant roses in full sun. Don't allow your rose plants to become stressed for moisture, and supply proper amounts of fertilizer at the right time of year. Vigorous, healthy-growing plants are much less prone to attack by pests and diseases.

Increase air circulation. Prune to keep plants open so air can circulate, allowing moisture to evaporate, and so light can reach all the foliage. This simple step will reduce many insects and diseases.

Water in the early morning hours. Plant leaves will dry before nightfall when cooler temperatures arrive, greatly reducing the chance of diseases such as black spot.

Keep the garden clean. Pull weeds as you see them. Rake up debris and destroy diseased plants and clippings to eliminate breeding areas for insects and diseases.

Encourage natural predators of pests. Eliminate or reduce use of pesticides so predatory insects such as ladybugs and lacewings can exist in your garden. Create combination plantings using other flowering plants that attract and shelter beneficial insects. For a list of some companion plants, see page 67. For more information on natural predators, see "Alternative Controls," page 156.

Use less toxic, alternative controls. An increasing number of nonchemical pest controls, including insecticidal soaps and horticultural oils, and biological controls such as *Bacillus thuringiensis* (Bt) are available. (See following.) Try these controls before resorting to the most-potent chemical means. Some mail-order sources of alternative pest controls can be found on page 39.

Trichogramma wasps parasitize the eggs of over 200 species of moths and butterflies.

Ladybird beetles (ladybugs) and their larvae feed on a variety of common rose pests, including aphids.

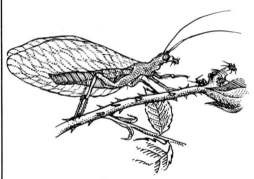

Lacewings and their larvae are effective beneficial insects, feeding on many rose pests.

General garden clean-up, including raking fallen leaves, removes disease organisms from the garden and eliminates shelter and breeding grounds for pests.

Aphids attack many plants, including roses, preferring to suck juices from new growth. Look for these pests in spring.

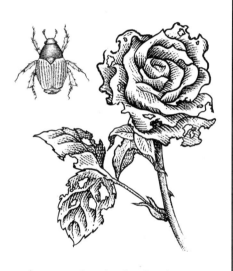

Japanese beetles feed on leaves and flowers of roses. They are most common in the eastern U.S.

Black spot disease is encouraged by wet, rainy weather. Help prevent by watering in early morning so leaves are able to dry before nightfall's cooler temperatures.

Alternative Controls

Here are some of the most effective alternative pest controls. Biological pest controls take advantage of living organisms that prey on plant pests.

Bacillus thuringiensis, commonly called Bt, is a bacterium that attacks and kills moth and butterfly larvae (caterpillars) but is harmless to humans. It is sold under several trade names; one of the most common is Dipel. A close relative, *Bacillus popilliae*, often called milky spore, attacks Japanese beetle grubs. However, it is more effective when sprayed over entire neighborhoods than when applied in a single garden.

Insect predators are natural enemies of plant pests. Many, including lacewings and ladybugs, occur naturally and can be encouraged to populate your garden and devour pests. Some can also be purchased through the mail and released in your garden. Among the most effective are trichogramma wasps. These tiny wasps don't bother humans but parasitize moth and butterfly larvae. Others include predatory mites, which feed on spider mites and sometimes thrips.

All insect predators require rather specific conditions to be most effective. Timing of their release is important, as are shelter and a food source after the pests have been taken care of. Before buying and releasing insect predators, it's wise to do some homework so you'll understand their needs. The mail-order sources for alternative pest controls listed on page 39 produce catalogs and other information that are excellent guides to selecting and maintaining a population of beneficial insects.

Botanical insecticides are controls derived from plant parts. Common botanical insecticides include *pyrethrum (pyrethroids* are synthetic pyrethrums; *pyrethrins* are natural products derived from pyrethrums), *neem, rotenone, rynia* and *sabadilla*. In general, these are considered *broad-spectrum* insecticides, which means they kill many types of pests. Some are more effective against certain pests than others. Once applied, they break down and lose their effectiveness quickly, so repeat applications are usually necessary. It is important to note that even though these are natural controls derived from plants, botanical insecticides are potent sprays that can be poisonous or cause allergic reactions. Follow all product label instructions carefully, as you would with chemical controls.

Insecticidal soaps interfere with the membranes of many types of pests, including aphids, scale and spider mites. You can buy them premixed or make your own soap spray by mixing 2 tablespoons of household liquid dishwashing soap in a gallon of water. Thoroughly spray the solution on the entire plant. Allow it to remain for an hour or two, then rinse the plant with clean water. Do not use insecticidal soaps or other soap sprays on plants that are in need of water or during periods of extreme heat.

Horticultural oils work because their coating action smothers insects and their eggs. *Dormant oils* are so named because they are sprayed on leafless plants in winter, while plants are dormant. Dormant oils are often combined with fungicides such as lime-sulfur to kill over-wintering disease organisms. *Summer oils* are sprayed when plants are in leaf during summer. Don't use summer oils on days when temperatures will rise above 85F.

Common Rose Pests and Controls

Pest & Symptom	Less Toxic Controls	Traditional Controls
Aphids—Tiny pear-shaped insects that suck plant juices, preferring new growth. Young leaves curl or become distorted. Most common in spring.	Knock them off with a strong jet of water. Or spray with insecticidal soap. Then let predators do their job (hollow aphid bodies are signs they are working). Pyrethrum and neem are effective botanicals.	Many chemicals, including malathion and acephate, are labeled for control of aphids.
Beetles—Hard-shelled insects that feed mostly on leaves and flowers. Japanese beetles can be a serious problem in certain regions, particularly in the East.	Hand-pick from plants and destroy. Use milky spore, a biological control. Pyrethrum and rotenone are effective botanicals.	Carbaryl and acephate.
Borers—Beetle or moth larvae that bore into cane, feed on tissues inside, eventually causing cane to wilt and die. Telltale sign is entry hole, usually found along dead cane.	Keep plant healthy and growing vigorously to prevent. Remove and destroy infested canes.	Few that are very effective.
Black spot—Small, fringed black spots on leaves. Leaves eventually turn yellow and drop. Common in areas with humid or wet summers.	Plant resistant varieties. Water in morning hours so leaves do not remain wet for extended periods. Prune to increase air circulation. Remove infected leaves. Try a baking soda and summer oil spray: (1 tablespoon baking soda plus 2 tablespoons oil in 1 gallon of water).	Triforine or phaltan.
Crown gall—Abnormally bumpy growth near the base of plant. Caused by soil-borne bacteria.	Avoid wounding plants when cultivating. Inoculate soil with bio-control *Agrobacterium radiobacter*.	Buy certified disease-free plants to prevent.
Downy mildew—Fungus, appears as white to grayish fuzz on undersides of leaves; yellow blotches on leaf tops. Common in cool, damp weather.	Plant disease-resistant varieties. Keep foliage dry as possible. Prune to increase air circulation.	Copper- or sulfur-based fungicides.
Nematodes—Microscopic worms that feed on roots and stunt growth. Small, round galls (bumps) can often be seen on the roots. Difficult to control.	Keep plants well fertilized. Apply chitin, ground-up shells, to the soil (ask your nurseryman about products that include it). Destroy infected plants.	None. Consult your cooperative extension office if you feel you have a serious infestation.
Powdery mildew—White, powdery fungus that distorts leaves and flowers.	Plant disease-resistant varieties in full sun. Prune for good air circulation. Try baking soda-oil mixture (see black spot). Spray foliage with anti-transpirant which forms a thin, waxy layer over the leaves making it harder for infection to get established.	Sulfur-based fungicides, triforine, benomyl.
Rust—Fungus that causes rust-colored spots on undersides of leaves. Most prevalent in western states.	Plant disease-resistant varieties. Water early in the morning so leaves dry quickly. Strip off infected leaves. Clean up fallen debris in winter.	Sulfur-based fungicides, triforine, plantvax.
Scale—Small, usually oyster-shelled insects that suck plant juices from stems and leaves.	Spray with horticultural oils when pest in mobile "crawler" stage. Try releasing parasitic wasps.	Orthene, malathion, carbaryl.
Spider mites—Microscopic, spiderlike pests that suck plant juices and turn leaves a stippled yellow. Inhabit undersides of leaves, often forming delicate webbing. Most common in hot, dry weather. Use magnifying glass to determine presence.	Avoid spraying chemicals that reduce natural predator levels. Keep foliage clean with water sprays or overhead watering. Release predatory mites. Spray with insecticidal soap, sulfur or horticultural oils.	Kelthane, if available.
Thrips—Minute, almost microscopic insect. Most common on white, pink or yellow roses early in summer. Distorts flowers causing brown spots. Distorts leaves.	Release green lacewings or predaceous mites. Spray with botanicals neem, pyrethrum or rotenone. Spray with insecticidal soap.	Orthene.
Viruses—Diseases usually transmitted by sucking insects such as aphids and leafhoppers. Cause distorted leaves with yellow mottling.	Prevent by purchasing certified, disease-free plants. Destroy severely infected plants.	Same as less toxic.

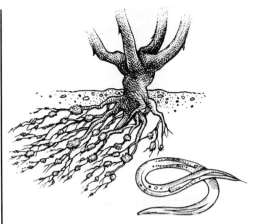

Nematodes are microscopic worms that damage roots. Infected plants show damage with stunted growth. Often, small round *galls* (bumps) can be seen on roots.

Powdery mildew is a white, powdery fungus on leaves and flowers, usually affecting new growth.

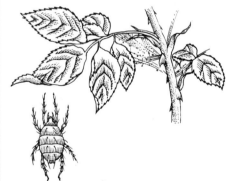

Spider mites thrive in dry, hot conditions. Use a magnifying glass to see them and their webbing, often on leaf undersides.

Thrips are tiny pests that distort flowers and leaves, causing brown spots. They prefer pink- or yellow-flowering roses.

Index

Numbers in bold italics refer to pages where photographs or illustrations appear.